Google is God: Technology and the Future of God

Google is God: Technology and the Future of God

Benton Fazzolari

Tarija-Sur Publishing

Thank you Dr. Frédéric Conrod & Dr. Steven Blakemore for your guidance and support throughout the process of writing this book.

Table of Contents

Introduction

Google is a Technological God

Google is a technological God whose media arbitrates virtually all forms of human activity. This was true of the Christian monotheistic God previous to Nietzsche's declaration of His death. Formerly, the metaphysical God (the ethical monotheistic God) served as the central mediator of human interaction and human states of being.

Humans created God and designed Him with several characteristics, such as omnipotence, omnipresence, omnibenevolence, and omniscience. Most importantly, human psychological drives informed the characteristics of God. Simply put, humans are psychologically driven to create a higher being or an Ideal self. Theologians extensively described that higher being. A psychoanalytic reading of "Google" explains the specific nature of God that aligns with, or serves as an extension to, the metaphysical God of the theologians, particularly the Scholastics.

Furthermore, "Google as God" manifests as an eventual outcome of scientific rationalism (or of the Enlightenment). Therefore, the tradition of rationalism embedded in Scholastic conceptions of

God serves to undergird the idea that Google is the logical extension of the Christian monotheistic (metaphysical) God. Hence, the discussion of this God from several of the central Scholastic theologians lays a foundation to define God from the Christian perspective. Therefore, the very method the Scholastics employed to understand the nature and attributes of God, actually results in what Nietzsche proclaims as the "Death of God." The continuum of thought "about God" from Descartes through Hegel, illustrates that God becomes impossible to explain as a metaphysical being and, eventually, becomes an entirely contradictory concept, which the scientific method displaces, altogether. The new God becomes science and manifests itself by technological advancement, which is epitomized by the contemporary entity, Google.

In addition, Freud's discussion of God explains the human drive to create God, and also serves as a bridge to Lacan's God *creatio ex nihilio*. Therefore, the shift of the metaphysical God, which morphs into the God of the Enlightenment, finally shifts, through Freud, to the God of modernity. The God of modernity loses its metaphysical explanation and becomes science and technology. The works of Heidegger and Historian Lewis Mumford explain the advent of the technological God as the extension (and replacement) of the metaphysical God. Also, McLuhan and Baudrillard provide the foundation for the analysis of Google's media and the eventual logical outcome of the technological God, which mirrors that of the metaphysical God: Death.

Therefore, the basic thesis of this book is straightforward. Humans create God, the western metaphysical God that almost conquered the planet. The contemporary technological God *will* conquer the planet. This book could be about a number of different technological Gods. Obviously, Amazon, Microsoft, Apple, Facebook, and others deserve a close study as Gods. The focus on Google relates to its goal to "organize the world's information and make it universally accessible and useful." The connotation of this goal abounds in alignment with God's characteristics. The death of God is also the death of Google. Its own expansion and proliferation will lead to the same death. The logical outcome of the method requires it to die. So, this book is about the second death of God.

Chapter 1

Humans Created God: Freud and Lacan

"God did not, as the Bible says, make man in His image; on the contrary . . . man, made God in his image."[1]

Sigmund Freud grew up in the small Catholic town of Freiberg, which housed a tiny percentage of Jewish residents. Hans Küng describes the anti-Semitism Freud faced as a child.[2] Freud learned of Judaism from his mother and attended Catholic Mass with his nanny.[3] Hence, he was extremely familiar with the monotheistic God who he critically examines in his book *The Future of an Illusion.* Freud denies the existence of God and explains why humans believe in Him. In addition, he makes specific claims that relate to the psychological reasons that pertain to the human creation of the ethical monotheistic God.

To understand Freud's notions of God requires a brief outline that relates to the evolution of "the father" from earlier times. Freud, who viewed Charles Darwin as a hero,[4] looks to Darwin's natural history to analyze the conflict between the son and the father. According to Darwin, "[Man] aboriginally lived in small communities, each with a single wife, or if powerful with several, whom he jealously guarded against all other men."[5] The "other men" included his sons. C. G. Schoenfeld explains, "When the growing sons excited the jealousy of their savage and brutal sire, they were killed, castrated, or driven from the primal horde . . . ultimately one of these sons succeeded to his father's position."[6] To Freud, the basis of the Christian God rests in this conception of the father.

Freud also offers the support of myths and fairy tales to illustrate his point. In *Moses and Monotheism,* he refers to Otto Rank's *The Myth and the Birth of the Hero* and concludes that a "Hero is a man who stands up manfully against his father and in the end victoriously overcomes him."[7] Therefore, the rivalry between the father and son began in primeval times. Despite the rivalry, Freud notes that the sons "loved and admired [the father,] too."[8] He continues, "After they [murdered] him . . . a sense of guilt made its appearance . . . felt by the whole group . . . [thus,] the dead father became stronger."[9]

Further, the sense of guilt remains within the unconscious. This remorse provides the initial drive to appease the dead father and to quell the feelings of guilt that lingers. In his essay "Death and Us," Freud constructs an uncomfortable representation of man that supports his theory. He writes, "The history of the world learned . . . [by] children is . . . a series of murders of peoples. The vague sense of guilt [remains] . . . which in some religions [is] primal guilt or original sin . . . [from] the men of prehistory."[10] Here, Freud explains the rise of the totemic religion.

Totemism is "the first religion in the history of mankind."[11] The origin of this religion "arose from the filial sense of guilt, in an attempt to allay that feeling . . . [and] all later religions are seen to be attempts at solving the same problem."[12] Essentially, a group selects a totem animal to worship and revere as well as sacrifice and kill. This represents the ambivalent feelings for the murdered primeval father.

Consequently, the entire system of religion becomes a necessary human construction and a compulsion toward a conception of the cosmos that removes this primeval guilt. Eventually the solution evolves from Totemism to monotheism, which "enthroned the father in a Kingdom of Heaven, thereby symbolically nullifying the unconscious guilt over the killing of the primal father."[13] Freud explains it in this way, "Paul, a Roman Jew . . . seized upon this feeling of guilt and correctly traced it back to its primeval source. This he called original sin . . . [Then] a Son of God . . . sacrificed himself and had thereby taken over the guilt of the world."[14] Furthermore, in Christianity, the primal father becomes divine or worshiped as a spiritual entity well after His murder. Freud concludes that the death of Christ demonstrates this historical fact.[15] In this fashion, Freud draws the timeline of the development from the father / son rival in primal hordes to the advent of the totemic religions and, finally, to Judeo-Christian monotheism. Accordingly, Freud declares, "God was the exalted father, and the longing for the father was the root of the need for religion."[16]

The primeval rivalry also serves as the foundation for Freud's Oedipus complex. During a period of self-analysis, Freud mentions the underlying precept of the complex, "I have found, in my own case, [the phenomenon] of being in love with my mother and jealous of my father, and I now consider it a universal event in early childhood."[17] Freud makes his own feelings a unanimous experience for all. He reinforces this in *The Interpretation of Dreams*, "The hypothesis I have put forward in regard to the psychology of children has an equally universal validity." Therefore, to Freud, all humans potentially live through the Oedipus drama in early childhood.

Freud's identification of the central drama in the life of a child coincides with his ideas about God. At the center of the drama lies conflict. The conflict with the father from the primeval period resides within the psyche of the child. *The Ego and the Id* offers a rich explanation of Freud's theory. It reads, "[When] the boy's sexual wishes in regard to his mother become more intense and his father is perceived as an obstacle to them: from this the Oedipus complex originates."[18] The primary aspect of the complex revolves around the "love and hate for the father, rather than between love for the mother and fear of the father."[19] Freud continues, "An ambivalent attitude to his father . . . [makes up] the content of the . . . Oedipus complex."[20]

Freud's connects his history and origin of God and religion to the personal development of the child. The young boy identifies with his father, but finds a growing desire for his mother. This narrative retains its psychological meaning through the girl, as well. Although some of the variables change, particularly with castration, the young girl enters a similar period of desire. Freud claims this in both positive and negative terms. Positive Oedipus complex in a boy bears the standard conflict and reverses for the girl. Negative Oedipus complex reverses the conflict in both boys and girls (desire for father and carries ambivalence for mother, etc.). In fact, Freud writes "Closer study usually discloses the Oedipus complex is . . . due to the bisexuality originally present in children."[21]

The boy must repress the feelings in order to "internalize" him as "an inner source of strength."[22] This serves as a requirement for a future healthy libido. Early in the boy's life (about the age of three), he must resolve this issue. Blass continues, "He gives up on an external beloved object [his mother] and attains an alternative internal one"[23] Even if resolved in early childhood, problems still potentially arise because, as Schoenfeld mentions, "The unconscious does not grow up . . . the fears that enter it during early childhood remain in their original infantile form."[24] As in the case of Oedipus the King, only later in life one may acquire the knowledge of the unconscious drives in one's own history. In other words, "The analysand must recreate his or her past and claim it arduously and painfully,"[25] through psychoanalysis. Castration functions as the other key element of the Oedipus complex. Again, conflict contributes to the psychical relationship with the father. This time it manifests in psychical fear. This fear enters the child when he first sees the female genitalia and discovers that she lacks a penis. Freud notes, "[A boy attributes] to everyone, including females, the possession of a penis . . . [until] he sees his little sister's genitals."[26] At this point, he experiences anxiety, which becomes the "source of the oedipal conflict."[27] Principally, the boy fears the punishment of castration by his father if he acts upon his desire for his mother. The boy has an opportunity to resolve the Oedipus complex as long as he "keeps the incest wishes well buried."[28] The boy does not act upon his sexual desire in exchange for the possibility of future sexual activity. Thus, he retains his penis and may resolve the desire for his mother. Incidentally, according to Naomi Morgenstern, "The girl . . . discovers her castrated state . . . [and] becomes an Oedipal subject, desiring what her father can give her, or so she thinks. She thus never successfully moves beyond the Oedipal moment."[29] Michael Kahn reinforces this when he writes, "The girl is apt to relinquish the Oedipus complex more slowly and less completely . . . [as] girls are not as motivated to destroy [it because] they are not under the threat of castration . . . [and] the mother does not seem as dangerous as father."[30]

Overall, the Oedipus complex, with its emphasis on the ambivalent childhood conflict with the father, supports Freud's entire perspective on

God and religion. To paraphrase Freud: when the boy grows up, he knows that he is stronger, but his understanding of the dangers in life have also grown. Therefore, he feels just as helpless and unprotected as he was in his childhood. He recognizes, too, that his father is helpless. He therefore remembers the image of the father of his childhood, whom he both loved and feared. He exalts the image into a deity.

Both the power of this image and the persistence of his need for protection sustain his belief in God. Certainly, these ideas existed before Freud. David Hume writes in 1757 in *The Natural History of Religion*, "No wonder, then, that mankind, being placed in such absolute ignorance . . . should immediately acknowledge a dependence on invisible powers . . . [that] we ascribe . . . thought, and reason . . . and the figures of men, in order to bring them nearer to a resemblance with ourselves."[31] Finally, Schoenfeld summarizes, "Men form God, not only of the master of the primal horde, but also . . . in the image of the father of childhood."[32] Therefore, the connection to primal religious drives in the creation of God and the contemporary clinging to God run consistently through Freud's conception of the Oedipal complex and God.

Freud's perspective of God and religion involves more. He defines God as an illusion. In terms of illusion, Ana-Marie Rizzuto points out that Freud considers "God and religion a wishful childish illusion."[33] Freud clarifies, "Men cannot remain children forever; they must in the end go out into 'hostile life' . . . We may call this 'education to reality.'"[34] To Freud, illusions are not the same as errors,[35] since they are "derived from human wishes."[36] Humans want to believe something to be true and, that certain something, may not be false. Freud offers the example when he writes, "One may describe as an illusion the assertion made by certain nationalists that the Indo-Germanic race is the only one capable of civilization."[37] Therefore, at the center of an illusion lies a wish. By comparison, Freud distinguishes its difference to the delusion. The delusion is in "contradiction to reality."[38] For example, when one believes that the earth is flat, that person is delusional because the flat earth contradicts objective reality. God's status as an illusion means that He may exist. Freud mentions, "That the Messiah will come and found a golden age is [very unlikely]."[39] Nonetheless, it is still an illusion, not a delusion. Therefore, Freud's enterprise encompasses the reasons why humans believe.

Furthermore, Freud asserts that humans create God to take away the terror of nature. Freud claims that human confrontation with nature led to the creation of Gods who controlled nature, such as the mythical Gods of ancient Greece. He writes, "A man makes the forces of nature not simply into persons . . . [He] gives them the character of the father . . . [and] he turns them into gods."[40] Death supplies one major element embedded within the terror of nature. Freud calls this the "cruelty of fate."[41] In order to overcome, or at least cope with, the overwhelming realization of the inevitability of death, humans create the illusion of life after death.

Freud observes, "Death itself is not extinction, is not a return to inorganic lifelessness, but the beginning of a new kind of existence which on the path of development to something higher."[42] Immortality offers a way to share intimacy with God as the Father like the child and his father.

This gave rise to the monotheistic God and further, the personal monotheistic God because one wants to be "his only beloved child."[43] This expands to entire "chosen peoples" and chosen "countries."[44] Of course, if one does not find favor with the father, one can be condemned to punishment.

Freud's concept of religion and God ties with the rise and creation of civilization, as well. With this advancement, humans prohibit certain instinctual wishes in return for certain protections and securities. Freud offers incest, cannibalism, and murder as examples.[45] In Totemism, which has "intimate connections with the later god-religions," the totem animals become "the sacred animals of the gods; and the earliest, but most fundamental moral restrictions, the prohibitions against murder and incest."[46] Again, the shift from the animal god to the human one relates to the "father-complex and man's helplessness and need for protection . . . [and] consist in the relation of the child's helplessness to the helplessness of the adult which continues it."[47] Consequently, the thousands of prohibitions and statutes in the Mosaic Law and other religious law set up a system of prohibitions and legalities that impinge on the basic intrinsic wishes of humankind, but in compromise offer humans the safety and fortification against the anxiety associated with the threats of murder, incest, and cannibalism.

Freud's assertions illustrate that God comes from our unconscious drive to overcome fear, guilt, and the natural world as well as to project the existence of an ideal transcendent being who humans can both love and fear. The metaphysical God served as a being who could help to resolve these human issues. The technological God comes from the same psychological drives to deal with the same ordeals from both the unconscious and the natural world. As a technological expression of human creativity, it overwhelms the natural world completely. Lacan theorizes the period called the mirror stage as a means to explain the moment during Freud's stages of psychosexual development that ignites the ego, which informs human fear and guilt, and contributes to the creation of God.

Lacan and *Creatio Ex Nihilio*

While Freud's theory of the human creation of God focuses on a psycho-anthropological analysis, Lacan utilizes Sausseurian linguistics to extend Freud's ideas about God. Therefore, with Lacan, the creation of God is still driven by the father and son relationship with fear and guilt in the unconscious, but he adds a psycho-philosophical explanation by altering the vocabulary to include terms that relate to human subjectivity and objectivity. Lacan also incorporates a few basic ideas from Christian theology in order to grasp the connections of human psychology to God.

The central theologians regard the center points of God's power as His ability to create from nothing (*creatio ex nihilio*) and the goodness of His creation. Lacan supports the idea of creation out of nothing. Lorenzo Chiesa and Alberto Toscano explain, "Lacan believes that there must logically be a 'moment' of creation *ex nihilo,* a point at which the symbolic emerges as an immanent consequence of the primordial real."[48] The "primordial real" or the pre-Symbolic "Real" proves inconceivable without the entrance of the signifying chain of the Symbolic. Essentially, the big Other or the transcendent signifier cannot manifest without the *structure* of language, and, henceforth, the primordial "Real" is (can be) God. To explain, the complete sign requires something to be signified by a signifier. It may include or refer to a referent, an actual object.

For Lacan, the role of the signifier bears the most significance. The signifier is the word. *Creatio ex nihilio* requires the word. Tad Delay notes, "The doctrine *creatio ex nihilio* holds such a prominent place in psychoanalysis, because at some point signifiers enter the world and make an irrevocable change in the subject."[49] Lacan explains by referencing John 1:1, "In the beginning was the Word, which is to say, the signifier."[50] Therefore, Lacan's Real exists before the Symbolic world that requires the Word to enter as the signifier. Clayton Crockett identifies where God comes from and how He is produced as "the region where [Lacan's] Real and Imaginary intersect"[51] and by paraphrasing Lacan, continues, "God is unconscious, and must be written into being."[65] Furthermore, to paraphrase Lacan, the unconscious does not exist; it insists.[52] Therefore, in terms of human subjectivity, the unconscious insists upon the emergence of God through the Symbolic register.

Lacan's Real exists regardless of human subjectivity, but also because of human subjectivity. He expounds, "Reality faces man, and that is what interests him in it, both as having already been structured and as being that which presents itself in his experience as something that always returns to the same place."[53] This demonstrates why, according to Slavoj Žižek, "only an atheist can believe."[54] Lacan first asserts the inversion. He states, "In the end, only theologians can be truly atheistic."[55] Michael Lewis offers this succinct explanation, he writes, "Creation is a way to indicate the absolute novelty of the signifier's functioning in the case of man, which is then precisely what needs to be explained or at least acknowledged to be insusceptible of explanation."[56] In response to the anti-creationism of Darwinism, Lacan clarifies that "[Evolution] merely assimilates culture to nature and thus denies the explanandum."[57] The connection of Lacan's Real to Augustine's assertion that "God is *is*"[58] bears the mark of Lacan's Real as a signifier whose state of being is simply His indescribable state of being without the word from the Symbolic order. Crockett confirms, "We never have access to the Real as Real, even in Lacan's late work, but only as already symbolized and imagined."[59]

Freud posits the Ego, Id, and Superego, while Lacan posits the Imaginary, Real, and Symbolic. Augustine and the like posit the Trinity of the Father, Son (Word), and Holy Spirit. Of course, Augustine admits, "Among all these things that I have said about that supreme trinity… I dare not claim that any of them is worthy of this unimaginable mystery."[60] Obviously, Augustine carefully engages this difficult topic and "at least acknowledged [it] to be insusceptible of explanation."[61] Regardless, Boethius, refers to the Word as "His [the Father's] Word" when he writes, "By His Word He . . . created the earth."[62] This confirms God's *creatio ex nihilio* and relates to the central requirement or the necessity of the Word in order for God the Father to create. Further, Mary T. Clark provides an analogy for clarity. She writes, "Just as in human communication the spoken word follows the mental word conceived by thinking, so Christ as the Word of God took flesh to communicate with human persons."[63] The act of thinking to produce a mental word (signifier) presents the essence of the unconscious insistence to articulate the nature of being with the presence of desire and subjective uncertainty. When Clark postulates Christ as the Word with the function to communicate with humans, Christ becomes a master-signifier.

To explain: a signifier does not need a referent and is necessarily replaced by other signifiers, but a master-signifier cannot be replaced by any other signifier. Basically, signifiers can be replaced by other signifiers and carry nothing inherent in their meaning. In fact, the signifier does not even require an actual object (noun) in order to serve as a signifier. This makes the concept of meaning problematic. Simply stated, the signifier only bears meaning within a society that conceives of specific signifiers in a similar way. Otherwise, when one uses a dictionary to look up a signifier, one finds other signifiers to explain the meaning of that signifier. Then one must look up those signifiers in an endless chain of words. Therefore, the Lacanian Symbolic exists as an undefined state of connections which hold society together and makes existence intelligible. The master-signifiers serve as a socially constructed exception because it only refers to itself. The famous example comes from Žižek, who extends Marx's commodity fetishism, to identify "money" as a master-signifier because "money as a commodity becomes self-referential, money is worth (signifies) money."[64] Obviously, money bears no meaning at all without the society that confirms its meaning. Similarly, the Christ who took flesh to communicate with humankind functions as a clear model of a master-signifier. In Lacanian terms, the Symbolic emerged from the Real to create the Imaginary.

Essentially, Lacan understands the presence of the signifier as the absence of another signifier. This coincides with the unconscious that underlies the entire Symbolic order of representation through the endless chain of signifiers. He asserts, "It is presence in absence and absence in presence."[65] Therefore, a signifier which does not appear, appears as a pseudolanguage of the unconscious. In semiology, the concept of the paradigm and the syntagm enunciates this difference depicted below.

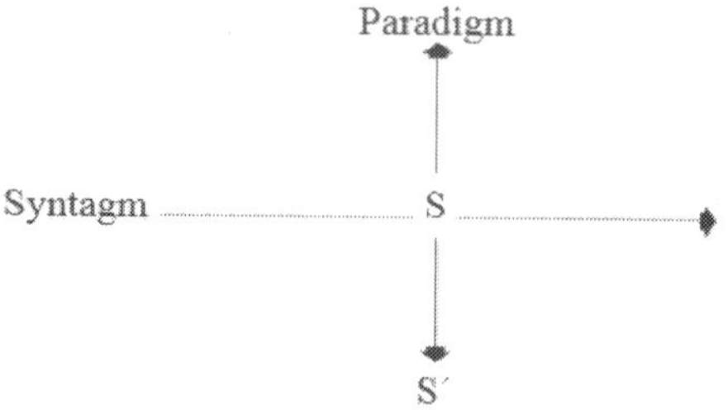

[66]

The diagram shows the endless options of paradigmatic signifiers. The "S" represents the manifest signifier, while the "S′" represents the latent signifier from the unconscious. The syntagmatic arrow flows in one direction as a universal pattern of language structure. The master-signifier cannot simply be substituted from the syntagm unlike all other signifiers. Thus, Christ, Jehovah, or Google serve as master-signifiers. Regardless, the presence of one signifier implies the absolute absence of another. The Symbolic register is that of the latent signifier in the unconscious. Hence, when Lacan asserts that "God is unconscious," he means that God, as a representation of the Real, cannot be grasped through the appearance of the Symbolic absence.

Rex Butler provides an example through interpreting Slavoj Žižek's discussion on the Apostle Paul. He writes, "For what [Paul] brings about is a situation in which the arguments used against Christ (the failure of His mission, His miserable death on the cross) are now reasons for Him (the sign of His love and sacrifice for use) . . . Paul doubles what is through the empty signifier, Christ's worthy mission, so that the very lack of success is success."[67] Simply, the absence of success becomes the presence of success. The term empty signifier (floating signifier) is a signifier without a referent. For instance, the signifier "bowl" shares a social meaning, which provides a solid denotation as a concrete object with essence, substance, and universal characteristics. Christ's mission does not. It means whatever it is supposed to mean in a circular or tautological fashion of explanation.

To reiterate Lacan's triad of human subjectivity, Julian Wolfreys summarizes, "Every time I speak, I draw on the signifier's constitution, the Symbolic, and seek to convey meaning, thereby constituting the Imaginary. In doing so, I draw on the 'historically' constituted discourse . . . of the Real . . . to which I have no direct access."[68] Richard Boothby adds, "The Real is not simply a designation of something unknown *external* to the individual. It inhabits the secret interior as well."[69] Lacan uses the example of the Borromean Knot:

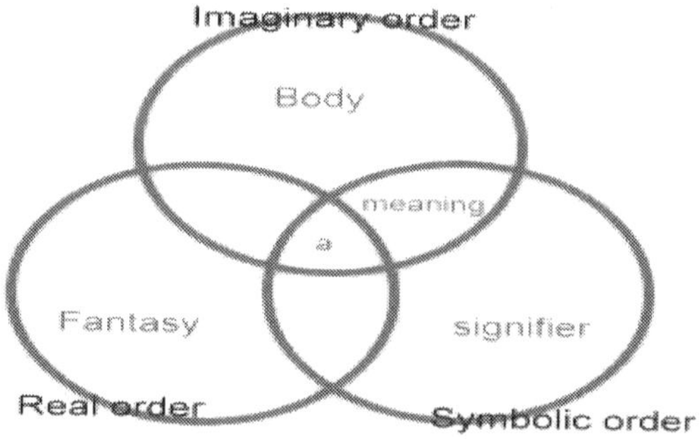

Wolfreys continues, "[The Borromean Knot] . . . is a way of linking three rings together in such a fashion that if you remove one, the other two fall apart."[70] In Lacan's words, "Within the phenomenon of speech we can integrate the three planes of the symbolic, represented by the signifier, the imaginary, represented by meaning, and the real, which is discourse that has actually taken place in a diachronic dimension."[71] Therefore, all three elements require the other for explanation. The overlap of the Imaginary and the Symbolic serves as the main point, which results in "meaning" of / for / about "the fantasy" of God. This fantasy is not simply something articulated in public discourse; it also swirls in the unconscious. An apt explanation of the Imaginary expressing the body comes from the communion of the body of Christ; an imaginary manifestation of the body when merged with the Symbolic provides meaning to the signifier and further moves to the fantasy of Christ's sacrifice.

To apply this to Google: God serves as the creator of the universe, as proposed by theologians; and Google serves as the creator, in contemporary applied science and technology through, literally, Sergei Brin and Larry Page. Both constitute human creations (*ex nihilio*) and both exit the axis of something with direct entry and sublime clarity into something that is Real in the Lacanian sense of the term. Moreover, the metaphysical God became complicated over time and became a being whose rational explanation eliminated the being, itself. Moreover, the intersection of the Imaginary and the Symbolic overwhelms the Real through meaning. Google shares this fate.

Human descriptions of God bring his primordial reality into existence through the Symbolic register of language (the Word) to create the perfect Imaginary entity or Father. This perfect entity is the ideal Ego of personal subjectivity ignited during the Mirror Stage. According to Lacan, the Mirror Stage occurs when the infant is six to eighteen months old. During this time, the infant repeatedly fixes his gaze upon his own image.[72] The infant conceives of itself as a human subject previous to the intense prohibitions enforced through societal norms. At this moment the ideal ego unconsciously initiates and articulates the desire to be like the Father and God. Basically, the human enters a life-long circuitry that moves along the path of an unconscious drive to be the ideal form of the self. Unable to fully achieve this ideal, the human creates God, the ideal ego.

Google is God

Both Freud and Lacan's overlapping conceptions of God, through psychoanalysis, will be explicitly connected to Google, throughout this book.

Chapter 2

The God Humans Created

Augustine of Hippo

Born in 354 AD, Augustine of Hippo merged the Greek philosophical tradition with the Judeo-Christian religious and scriptural traditions. His range of discourses includes commentary on original sin and the Trinity. He describes a God similar to other famous Church Fathers, Scholastics, and theologians. To him, God is a perfect being in every possible way whose central attributes include omnipotence, omnipresence, omnibenevolence, and omniscience. These qualities work together and reinforce each other to the point where, in rational terms, God must exist above, apart, and beyond all other creatures in the universe as the supreme almighty being.

In *The City of God, Volume 2,* Augustine directly mentions God's omnipotence. He writes, "He who by His . . . omnipotence distributes to everyone his own portion, is able to make good use not only of the good, but also of the wicked."[73] All of God's qualities connect to His goodness or (omni)benevolence. His omnipotence supplies the energy to distribute good. According to Augustine, God's power enables Him to do miraculous things. Augustine notes that "even though the body has been all quite ground to powder . . . it shall not be beyond the omnipotence of the Creator; no, not a hair of its head shall perish."[74] The power that God exhibits correlates with His acts of creation, and His ability to maintain life for His creation.

God's omnipotence also involves the creation of law, both eternal and temporal. Therefore, God holds the ultimate power in how objects of the universe, including humans, operate. To paraphrase, Augustine claims that those who love eternal things live under eternal law, while those who love temporal things live under the temporal law.[75] So humans, through God's gift of free will, can choose what things to love, whether eternal or temporal. Therefore, free will fits into God's creation and offers humans the ability to choose right or wrong; but humans must choose correctly. Augustine carries an almost mystical conception of the omnipresence of God. Stanislaus Grabowski explains that to Augustine, God is clearly "Being unqualified: He simply is."[76] In his *Expositions on the Psalms*, Augustine claims that "God is *is*, even as the good of goods is good."[77] By the phrase "God is *is*," Augustine conveys "to us [that] God's eternal immutable existence or presence . . . is completely independent of our chronological framework of time regarding the past, present, and future."[78] This concept of God's essence and nature repeats throughout the writings of the Church Elders and the Scholastics. God simply reigns as a separate entity entirely outside (*and inside*) of every part of the created universe. Human time lives on the outside of

God because human conceptions, such as time, reflect human subjectivity which requires a state of being or action. God's nature encompasses all being, or He is being. Furthermore, "God is or exists everywhere in the totality of reality or immensity of space."[79]

Grabowski adds, "Omnipresence is proper to God alone in relation to place. Eternity and omnipresence are attributes that deny limitations of time and space."[80] So to think of God in the realm of the human place incorrectly identifies the nature of God's omnipresence. Augustine clarifies, "Let us not try to bring God to place . . . if He were in place, He would not be God. God is present in, and to the whole universe in such a manner as to be whole in the whole universe."[81] Hence, God's omnipresence distinctly detaches God's nature from that of the human. So Augustine explains that time and place for God means beyond time and place.

As it concerns omniscience, Augustine answers questions that pertain to God's (fore)knowledge and, again, human free will. Augustine defends the compatibility of foreknowledge (an element of omniscience) and human free will against the likes of Cicero and the Stoics who assert that if God knows all, then human free will becomes impossible. Firstly, Augustine, like the future theologians, asserts that the essence of God involves knowledge of everything. He connects this to creation. He writes, "Of all visible things, the world is the greatest; of all invisible things, the greatest is God."[82] He then adds, "The [eternal] wisdom of God, by whom all things were made, was there [for the creation]."[83] So God's creation lends credence to the claim of His omniscience.

Additionally, Augustine affirms that the religious mind chooses both divine foreknowledge and human free will by the faith of piety.[84] Those who believe properly in God believe that "God knows all things before they come to pass, and that we do by our free will whatsoever we know and feel to be done by us."[85] With that established, Augustine explains that God does not control the wills of people. He makes a distinction between the will of the good and of the evil. He proclaims, "[God] is the bestower of all powers, not of all wills; for wicked wills are not from Him, being contrary to [His] nature."[86] This includes the evil wills of wicked angels and of wicked humans. For instance, Satan the Devil chose of his own free will to defy God, but his will held limited power. God's foreknowledge allowed Him to foreknow that Satan would have the power to sin, and that he *would* sin.[87] Regardless of specific choices, free will exists as a gift from God and does not conflict with His omniscience. Therefore, God's omniscience contains His goodness, His creation, and His foreknowledge as it originates within God's essential nature or natural essence.

God's omnibenevolence comingles and reinforces His other central attributes. Augustine announces, "His greatness is the same as His wisdom; for He is not great by bulk, but by power; and His goodness is the same as His wisdom and greatness, and His truth the same as all those things."[88]

All of these attributes coincide as "God as essence," not necessarily as God's substance. Augustine's concept of God's goodness in relation to His other attributes represents a particular and vital idea on the nature of God. Augustine explains, "It is an impiety to say that God subsists, and is a subject to His own goodness, and that this goodness is not a substance or rather essence and that God Himself is not His own goodness, but that it is in Him as in a subject; . . . God alone should be called essence."[89] Basically, God is not a subject as humans are subjects, and to say that God is a subject that has goodness within is inaccurate because God is goodness. It is not in him. It is Him. In context, this assertion must be understood in terms of the perfect and separate God; thus, it makes discourse on God impossible without occasionally positing God as a subject in order to explain the particulars of His nature.

As mentioned earlier, God utilizes his power for good to the point that those who are evil are still always good. For instance, certain men who became prideful and commit evil deeds against God are given the free will to choose to be evil. Aside from the goodness God gives for offering his creation free will, His creation retains an element of goodness simply because God is goodness and anything God creates is through His goodness and, therefore, must also be good. Augustine emphasizes this point when he writes, "For this amounts to finding fault with God's work, because man is an entity of God's creation."[90] God did not create evil, and the evil that does exist did not come from God. So nobody should find fault with any of God's creation.

God made everything good. This pinpoints the central goodness of God. In simple terms, God only creates good, and so anything evil can be described as only being less good. Augustine uses the term greater good to provide a spectrum of goodness through God. He writes, "Every actual entity is therefore good; a greater good if it cannot be corrupted, a lesser good if it can be."[91] By positing God as perfectly good (omnibenevolent) above all else, Augustine comes to the challenge of evil and produces a cogent argument that defines evil as a "lesser good." Of course, Augustine also rationalizes a potential contradiction in God's nature of evil and punishment for evil.

Anselm of Canterbury

Anselm of Canterbury composed the extremely popular and influential Ontological Argument for the existence of God between the years 1077-1078 AD. In his *Proslogion* he posits that "God is that which nothing greater can be thought."[92] The central characteristics of this entity, of which nothing can be greater, include omnipotence, omniscience, etc. In fact, these characteristics form the essence of God. In other words, only God can have these characteristics and that is what God is and what everything else is not. Anselm even states that "everything that exists, except for you alone, can be thought not to exist."[93] This further separates the unique and exclusive attributes within the being of God.

To relay God's omnipotence, Anselm produces a basic piece of logic that hinges upon God's perfection. If one starts with the idea that God is perfect, then to attach "omni" qualities to God requires little argument. Anselm asks hypothetically, "But how are you omnipotent if you cannot do everything?"[94] God's power manifests itself in will, action, and creation. All of His power causes good to all. For example, Anselm declares "O good God, good to the good and to the wicked . . . your goodness is incomprehensible."[95] So God's omnibenevolence rests in His goodness to all people, and His incapability to do anything evil.

Since God is a perfect being, so is his knowledge. He is omniscient. This pertains to understanding of all creation. Anselm writes, "If wisdom in the knowledge of created things is desirable, how desirable is the wisdom that created all things from nothing."[96] God's creation provides the evidence for his omniscience. This entails a universal knowledge encompassing everything or as Brown describes it: "The eternal God knows all events as a timeless observer of them."[97] Anselm wrestled with the potential contradiction of divine foreknowledge and human free will. Eileen Serene offers an example to explain Anselm's reconciliation of the two conflicting ideas. He writes:

> If it is true that Socrates is sitting at *t1* , what God knows prior to *t1* is that Socrates will sit

> then, and what he knows afterwards is that he did sit then. Since the only moment when God knows the truth that Socrates is sitting at *t1* is *t1* itself, his knowledge is simultaneous with the act of sitting, and this knowledge cannot be a prior cause of it.[98]

Therefore, God's omniscience does not interfere with Socrates's decision to sit. Socrates freely sat of his own will despite God's knowledge that Socrates will sit before Socrates actually sits. Later Anselm explicitly explains the nature of God's omnipresence. He writes, "The supreme Nature cannot exist finitely, at some place or time."[99] The law of space and time apply to the "beings which so exist in space and time."[100] This includes humans. God is different.

Anselm reasons: "The Substance which creates and is supreme among all beings, which must be alien to, and free from, the nature and law of all things which itself created from nothing, is limited by no restraint of space or time."[101] Thus, God resides "in every place at every time."[102] Moreover, to quote Hud Hudson, "Omnipresence for Anselm, then, is ultimately reducible to a kind of knowledge, immediate and localized for every region."[103] This assertion remains consistent with his central assertion that "God is that which nothing greater can be thought."[104] Since none can be greater thought in terms of time and space, God must be beyond or transcend time and space.

St. Thomas Aquinas

Simply known as Thomas, St. Thomas Aquinas was a thirteenth century friar who wrote prolifically. In his sprawling volume concerning the nature of God, *Summa Theologica,* Thomas works to defend the characteristics of God against various objections. He offers replies to the assertion that God is not omnipotent.[105] Thomas claims that "God's omnipotence is particularly shown in sparing and having mercy . . . [and] he freely forgives sins."[106] So to Thomas, power does not mean strength only, but also the ability to do something or to make something happen.

In this case, it is the ability to manifest mercy to humans. This illustrates that God's omnipotence correlates to God's omnibenevolence. Thomas also overlaps omnipotence with omniscience when he writes, "Hence God's omnipotence includes, in a way, universal knowledge and providence."[107] Thomas also discusses omnipotence as to God's power in what is possible or impossible. He writes, "Those things which it belongs to God alone to do immediately, as, for example, to create . . . are said to be possible in reference to a higher cause."[108] God's omnipotence makes it possible to create. However, Thomas carefully notes that it is illogical to object to God's omnipotence with absolutely impossible ideas: "For such cannot come under the divine omnipotence, not because of any defect in the power of God, but because it has not the nature of a feasible or possible thing."[109] God's power to create offers a significant claim. To create means to make something new or cause something to exist. According to Thomas, this requires the power of God, particularly when it involves a higher purpose. This higher purpose involves creation that encompasses all things, including humans.

Thomas presents God's omnipotence as God's power to show mercy and the power to create. He does not equate omnipotence with political power or the type of power a government or corporation imposes or uses in relation to humans. He declares that "[God] has the governance of the whole universe . . . [and] in place of power, He has omnipotence . . . [and] the government of all things."[110] This illustrates a slight distinction in Thomas's perception of God's omnipotence from the understanding of concentrated power as a force, so commonly proposed.

To Thomas, God's omnipotence means the power to actively do something, like create or forgive, not necessarily, the power to enforce rules or dictate ways of being. But, nonetheless, God does have the ultimately understood role as the supreme governor of the entire universe. His governing of the universe is simply a fact related to his essence and a logical necessity based upon his creation of the universe.

Thomas also comments on God's omnipresence. He writes, "It belongs to God to be present everywhere, since He is the universal agent, His power reaches to all being, and hence He exists in all things."[111] Again, Thomas posits what lives within God's very nature. God can be nothing but omnipresent. No action by any other agent can exist without or separate from the agency of God. God's omnipresence overlaps with His omnipotence because God has the power to create and without God's creation, there would be no "being." Furthermore, there would be no "things" in which to exist. Thomas emphasizes that beings, such as angels (who come from God), cannot be in "the same place at the same time,"[112] like God. They can only be sent by God to one place through God's authority. So an angel "is 'here' in such a manner as not to be "'there'"[113] This distinction highlights the complete omnipresence of God as an exclusive attribute.

Another distinction which nuances Thomas's claim on God's omnipresence consists of His being in all things instead of around all things as an outside presence. Thomas mentions, "God is neither circumscriptive nor definitively there, because He is everywhere."[114] Circumscriptive serves as a key term because it implies that God does not enclose or set up boundaries around places, events, or people. In His nature he is in the place, event, or people. This presents a division in God's omnipresence and omniscience. God does not know all because he is everywhere (in everything). He knows everything because it is in his essence to know everything.

Thomas addresses God's omniscience. He writes, "In God there exists the most perfect knowledge."[115] This makes it obvious that God cannot be wrong because what He knows is perfect. In contrast to human knowledge that merely manifests itself as a quality or attribute of the human who learns something. God's knowledge resides in His essence as He "knows all by one simple act of knowledge."[116] To be more specific, Thomas separates intellect, the object understood, the intelligible species, and God's understanding, to declare that to (or in) God, these are "one and the same."[117] So "His act of understanding must be His essence and His existence"[118] This central theme that concerns God in Thomas repeats throughout his writing. Basically, if God is God, then his knowledge is perfect, and He is omniscient.

Within this realm of perfect knowledge exists the knowledge of the universal and the particular. Thomas's logic goes as follows: "If therefore the knowledge of God regarding things other than Himself is only universal and not special, it would follow that His understanding would not be absolutely perfect . . . [and] to know a thing in general and not in particular, is to have imperfect knowledge."[119] Thus, God's perfection within His essence incorporates His perfection in His knowledge. Thomas offers an analogy: "For the knowledge of God is to all creatures what the knowledge of the artificer is to things made by his art."[120] This means that God, as the creator, knows all things universally, as in the entire human body, for example; and particularly, as in each part of the human body. This is so because of his power to create, his will, and his goodness, and his knowledge; all of which are perfect.

According to Thomas, God's omnibenevolence strongly ties to God's will. He asserts that "God loves all existing things."[121] He loves all existing things because His "will is the cause of all things."[122] So God, through his power, willed the universe and all things in it with love. God's inspiration to create illustrates his love. He did not create all things and then love of things. He brought all things into existence motivated by love. Existence represents the criteria of God's love for the thing / object. The object's existence represents, in material and physical form, God's love or as Thomas describes it, "A thing has existence, or any kind of good, only inasmuch as it is willed by God. To every existing thing, then, God wills some good."[123] This makes God's love unique from human love.

Human love relies on the object's existence before the object can be loved. In fact, the human is also an object in relation to God. Thomas utilizes a reversal of God's love to understand human love as different. He claims that "[Human] will is not the cause of the goodness of things, but is moved by it as by its object, our love, whereby we will good to anything, is not the cause of its goodness; but conversely its goodness . . . calls forth our love."[124] Humans cannot infuse goodness into an object. Human love adds nothing to the object itself. By God bringing the object into existence, through love, the object contains goodness, which then inspires humans to love the object. So, for example, a human may love their spouse, but that love does not infuse goodness into the spouse. The spouse is already infused with goodness because God brought her into existence out of love.

Finally, God carries essential goodness; his creation does not carry essential goodness. His creation is good because He created it, or goodness and being are the same.[125] To elaborate, with God, there are no accidents, only what He has willed. Humans display an element of goodness, but goodness is not an essential quality of humanity. Human goodness only knows reality through God. Thomas mentions, "Whatever belongs to others accidentally belongs to Him essentially."[126] Accidentally, in this context, implies something that occurs outside of one's essential character or "essence" or something that is "superadded."[127] He emphasizes, "He Himself alone is essentially good."[128]

Religious thinkers like Augustine, Anselm, and Thomas offer a specific depiction of God that includes elements of His nature or essence, which support the separate and perfect being found in the ontological argument for the existence of God. Omnipotence clearly functions as the central attribute that informs His other attributes. God's power to create manifests in the benevolence of creation. All things created share God's goodness. Through God's benevolent power, He knows everything, including the future, but because He loves his creation, He allows them to freely choose in conscious life. God's omniscience links to His omnipresence. The creation illustrates His power and love, which constitutes His knowledge, and finally, which establishes His universal presence. God is everywhere because He created everything and He is, therefore, in all (or part of) creation. As the separate deity, He resides outside of time and place and exists alone as the single contingent being (He is being) in the universe. To quote Augustine, "God is *is*."[129]

In terms of the technological God, Google, the essential points to grasp involve the theological claims that concern the metaphysical God's all-encompassing power, presence, love, and knowledge. One complete God carries all of these attributes within its essential being. This God mediates all human activity. This God provides humans with free will and, yet, will offer consequences for the exercise of free will. Therefore, God represents a contradictory being. But His contradictions absorb into His entire being. Google's all-encompassing Godly role in contemporary human life mirrors the role of the metaphysical God as described by the theologians.

Freud and Lacan provide the explanation for the creation of God, and the above theologians specifically describe the characteristics of the God humans created. Both the psychological motivation for the creation of God and the specific attributes of God will be explicitly connected to Google, throughout this book.

Chapter 3

The Death of the Metaphysical God

The psychologically motivated development of the metaphysical God, through reason, results in Nietzsche's declaration that "God is Dead."[130] Nietzsche's ideas serve to pinpoint this transformation or shift. This includes the conception and progression of the metaphysical God from the perspectives of philosophers: Descartes, Kant, and Hegel. Mark Wrathall notes that "The decline of the metaphysical God was perhaps first noted when Pascal declared that the God of the philosophers was not the God of Abraham, Isaac, and Jacob."[131] Henceforth, Nietzsche signals the endpoint of God through the philosophical tradition based in rationalism.

To repeat, in *The Gay Science* Nietzsche proclaims, "God is dead."[132] This statement receives a great share of misinterpretation in popular culture. It also bears ambivalence as a metaphor. For instance, Robert Pippen reasons, "If there had been a god, we could not have killed him. If we could have killed him, he could not have been a god."[133] In context, Nietzsche's claim certainly rests on his own atheism as well as on the rising power of scientific rationalism. Despite this, his declaration was never meant to support the project of scientific rationalism. To confirm, Andre Groenewald and Johan Buitendag claim that Nietzsche looked "for a concept of God that transcends modern atheism and theism."[134] Further, they note, "Nietzsche distanced himself from . . . theologians . . . and the superficial atheism of the natural scientists."[135] Therefore, Nietzsche's claim involves more than simply the (un)believability of God through the failure of metaphysical reason. It also involves a distinct loss for humanity and a potential slip into nihilism.

Nietzsche's claim rests upon the idea that "The Christian religion was no longer the presupposition of civilization."[136] Groenewald and Buitendag concur: "Theology was in crisis because humanity, rather than God, had become the center of attraction."[137] However, Nietzsche does not necessarily see the death of God with optimism like many of the scientific rationalists because "Nietzsche sees the death of God to lead to the problem of disenchantment that the ultimate significance of our lives (previously understood in terms of our relationship to God) has been replaced by an essentially insignificant world (of mere causal interaction)."[138] Thus, Nietzsche perceives God ambivalently as an idea under construction for millennia. Nevertheless, the developing idea, in the minds of humankind, dies.

To elaborate, Nietzsche believes that ideas impose influence upon humanity in the form of values. Therefore, in this way, God was alive to Nietzsche; alive in the sense that God strongly informed the point-of-view of individuals in society. Heidegger clarifies Nietzsche's position concerning God as an imposition of values. He explains, "The essence of value lies in the point-of-view. Value means that which is in view for a seeing that aims at something . . . the aim in view is value. Values as points-of-view are conditions of preservation and enhancement."[139] Basically, humans carry a particular point-of-view embedded with specific values and aims to preserve and enhance the point-of-view (values) in order to engage in "becoming," which is Nietzsche's "will to power."[140] In *Will to Power*, Nietzsche says, "Values and their changes are related to the increase in power of that which posits them."[141] The metaphysical Christian God informed the values in the point-of-view of the Church who exerted energy to preserve and enhance its ideas (the Christian God). Hence, if the idea of God infiltrates the vantage points of individuals (through force or otherwise) then the virtual nature of God's existence maintains agency within the structure of society, and God exists. Thus, God can die, and humans can kill God.

This alludes to human subjectivity and epistemology. For instance, to Nietzsche, rational proof of the existence of God proves worthless and unnecessary. Furthermore, Nietzsche realizes that "in the knowing subject the idea of knowledge outside the borders of the subject was not possible; that no truth, no certainty and no knowledge existed outside the knowing subject."[142] Therefore, human subjectivity allows one to kill an idea and create new ideas for "becoming" in the world. The new point-of-view (values) of one human subject can transform the individual through a revaluing of transient human beliefs. Michael Lackey follows this idea when he writes, "For in killing God . . . [Nietzsche] has set into motion the creative self-overcoming of 'self' which will empower individuals to expand the borders of what was once known as the human."[143] Nietzsche's claims carry value for individual liberation against the oppressive dictates of the Christian theologians, but there also exists an underside to his claims.

To read further in *The Gay Science*, the context becomes apparent. Nietzsche writes, "We have killed him! How shall we console ourselves, the most murderous of all murderers? . . . The holiest and the mightiest that the world had hitherto possessed, has bled to death under our knife."[144] Clearly, murder occurs. How did humans murder God? To clarify, Heidegger writes, "The terms 'God' and 'Christian God' in Nietzsche's thinking are used to designate the suprasensory world in general. The realm of the suprasensory has been considered since . . . the late Greek and Christian interpretation of Platonic philosophy, to be true and genuinely real."[145] Hence, a singular God does not die; rather the entire loss of confidence in the claims of Western metaphysics renders God meaningless.[146]

Therefore, the more appropriate questions are: Who killed the metaphysical God and how? In order to answer this question adequately, one must look at the progression of philosophical thought in relation to God from Descartes to Nietzsche. The philosophical project of reason, especially including metaphysics, killed God. Therefore, Nietzsche served as an endpoint to a long tradition that worked to explain the nature of existence and being while incorporating suprasensory concepts. With the spiritual or immaterial realm as a foundation and the advent of scientific means to access knowledge, the God-believing philosopher found it necessary to expand the nature of God to the point where God becomes unbelievable, contradictory, and untenable.

Furthermore, when Nietzsche declares "God is Dead," he worries about a nihilistic world. He writes, "The highest values are devaluing themselves."[147] Because the central theologians posit God as a perfect being (highest values) who could not maintain that illusion, *that* God dies. More precisely, the theologians and the God-believing rationalists could not maintain this illusion by the use of reason. Heidegger asks, "Oh what are the highest values if they do not simultaneously render secure the warrant and the ways and means for a realization of the goals posited in them?"[148] So, without the elevation of the ideal embedded in the metaphysical God, a form of passive nihilism could permeate human values. Henceforth, some ideal had to replace the metaphysical God.

Descartes

To clarify, the natural endpoint of utilizing reason to explain the ideal ("omni") God, eliminates God. In *The Birth of Tragedy* Nietzsche asserts how reason "coils around itself and finally bites its own tail."[149] For instance, Descartes clings to the existence of the Christian God while he emphasizes the use of reason to access truth. In his monumental text, *A Discourse on Method,* he demonstrates this attempt when he writes, "For it is not a dictate of reason that what we thus see or imagine is in reality existent, but it plainly tells us that all our ideas or notions contain in them some truth. For otherwise, it could not be that God, who is wholly perfect and veracious, should have placed them in us."[150] Aside from being a reworking of Anselm's ontological argument, his central assumptions include the existence of God, His perfection, and His divine omniscience. Of course, Descartes witnessed Galileo's condemnation from the Church, which resulted in his momentary notion of never publishing again.[151] Nonetheless, Descartes still tries to reconcile God and reason in *Meditations on the Foundations of Philosophy,* which according to Küng, "provoked vigorous opposition on the part of Catholic and Protestant theologians."[152] Apparently, the theologians of the time saw their God shifting away from the Scholastic or even Reformed God to the hyper-rational God.

Regardless, Descartes argues, "from the very fact that I can derive from my thoughts the idea of something, it follows that all that I clearly and distinctly recognize as characteristic of this thing does in reality characterize it . . . It is certain that I find in my mind the idea of God, of a supremely perfect being . . . and I recognize that an actual and eternal existence belongs to his nature."[153] In the midst of arguing for the *certainty* of God's existence, Descartes problematizes the very entity he aims to prove. His four rules lead to methodological doubt or an advanced / extreme doubt, the penultimate to outright skepticism. If one reads the subtext of (or deconstructs) statement sixteen in *Principles of Philosophy*, the death of God seems inevitable from the natural or logical outcome of reasoning about God. It states, "Hence, at times when we are not intent on the contemplation of the supremely perfect being, a doubt may easily arise as to whether the idea of God is not one of those which we made up at will."[154] Ironically, this statement answers a self-created arbitrary objection to God's existence. Küng concludes, "With Descartes, European consciousness . . . reached an epochal turning point . . . the medieval way of reasoning from certainty of God to certainty of self is replaced by the modern approach: from certainty of the self to certainty of God."[155] Descartes's reversal helps Nietzsche to declare the murder of God because it solely relies on human subjectivity manifested in rational thought. In other words, belief in the existence of the self (personal human subject) precedes and validates the existence and subsequent belief in God, rather than belief in God confirming the existence of the self.

Kant

Kant provides even more assistance to Nietzsche. Although Kant asserts an argument to support belief in God, he offers a devastating refutation of the three central arguments proposed for the existence of God. In the section entitled "Transcendental Dialectics" from the *Critique of Pure Reason,* Kant refutes "traditional proofs of the existence of God."[156] They are the ontological, the cosmological, and the physico theological arguments.[157] Anselm's ontological argument proposes that "God is that which nothing greater can be thought." Kant rejects this reasoning. He asserts, "The concept of a highest being is a very useful idea in many respects; but just because it is merely an idea it is entirely incapable all by itself of extending our cognition in regard to what exists."[158] To clarify Kant, "Logical possibility of the concept of an absolutely necessary being is not the same as real possibility; a jump from the former to the latter is not acceptable."[159] Simply put, Kant does not agree that one can "define things into existence"[160] or "one cannot, by adding existence to a concept that has application contingently if at all, get a concept that is necessarily exemplified."[161] Therefore, Kant strongly critiques one of the most famous and well-regarded proofs of God's existence within his framework of rationality. Again, reason itself eliminates God.

Kant then refutes the cosmological argument for the existence of God. The cosmological argument claims that since the world and the universe exist, some-thing first causes it to be. Kant argues, "It is really only the ontological proof from mere concepts that contains all the force of proof in the so-called cosmological proof . . . perhaps leading us only to the concept of a necessary being, but not so as to establish this concept in any determinate thing."[162] Kant uses the term "mere concepts" frequently in his *Critique.* This phrase counters empirical evidence because a mere concept only offers assumptions made from reason rather than from empirical / sensory experience. Kant already criticizes the ontological argument and sees the cosmological argument as an extension of the ontological, since the concept of the being does not necessitate the being's existence in objective reality. The earth and the universe may exist concretely as objects to a subjective mind, but that does not prove the existence of a being outside of the observer who precedes the entire physical realm. Kant argues, "The inference from the impossibility of an infinite series of causes given one upon another to a first cause, which the principles of the use of reason itself cannot justify our inferring within experience, still less our extending this principle to somewhere beyond it (into which the causal chain cannot be extended at all)."[163] Therefore, the cosmological argument for the existence of God diminishes in Kant's view. Also, since Kant declares that reason "cannot justify our inferring with experience," he paradoxically challenges reason with reason and hence challenges the existence of God with reason.

Finally, Kant refutes the physico theological argument for God's existence. This argument explains, "There are clear signs of order and purposiveness everywhere in the world . . . [and] God is understood as that all perfect, highest cause, the architect whose existence explains the order we see."[164] Again, Kant refutes this proof for God's existence with the same reasoning that refutes the cosmological argument. He writes that the physico theological argument "elevates itself from magnitude to magnitude up to highest of all, rising from the conditioned to the condition, up to the supreme and unconditioned thing."[165] The contingent first cause cannot simply appear in concrete or objective reality because things in concrete or objective reality exist empirically. Kant does not support the existence of something unconditioned because of the appearance of order among those things that are conditioned. Obviously, this evidence does not cover all of the nuances of the proofs of God's existence or Kant's refutation of the proofs; but this evidence supports Nietzsche's claim that theological and later philosophical reasoning (and/or metaphysics) causes the inevitable death of God and supports his claim in *The Gay Science* that "We have killed Him."[166]

Despite refuting God's existence, Kant still clings to the belief in God founded upon human reason. To Kant, belief in God does not require absolute proof of God's existence. Allen Wood clarifies, "[The] concept of a supremely real being arises naturally and even inevitably [through reason]."[167] The central arguments for God's existence illustrates Wood's point, but, as seems obvious, this does provide absolute theoretical evidence. Thus, Kant feels that the human faculty of reason allows humans to reach a vague notion of God, but humans still have "no concept at all of what it is in itself."[168] Kant calls this thing we know

"Something."[169] The evidence that reason apprehends this "Something" rests in the proliferation of ideas over centuries that pertain to this "Something." Therefore, humans reason God into necessary belief, but not into necessary existence.

Finally, Kant completes his belief in God when he cites the requirement of belief for morality. He proposes, "The highest good in the world is possible only in so far as one assumes a supreme cause of nature that has a causality conforming to the moral attitude."[170] Groenewald and Buitendag summarize, "To Kant humans were moral beings that had to perform certain moral duties. God was not an object, but an idea of the rational mind. The idea of God rested on . . . practical reason's willing of the good and its acknowledgement of moral law."[171] Therefore, Kant separates practical reason and pure reason. From practical reason, God exists as an idea for the moral benefit and duty of human beings. Understandably, to Nietzsche, whose views on morality differ from Kant's, this line of reasoning serves to murder God rather than to maintain God. In fact, Kant, in his *Critique of Judgment* concludes, "This moral argument is not meant to offer any objectively valid proof of the existence of God."[172] The natural progression of the field of metaphysics (and / or reason) kills God who represents the entire suprasensory world.

Hegel

Hegel further murders God. One major concern of Hegel involves God as a being. Humans exist as beings. A being exhibits traits like power, knowledge, love, and presence. In fact, God exemplifies these qualities. However, Hegel's God differs in terms of the noun "being." John Caputo explains that "Hegel prepared the way for the insight that just as God is not a being that steers things from above, neither is God some immanent guiding force situated here below."[173] Thus, God loses the omni-attributes assigned to Him by the Church Fathers because only physical beings articulate and are associated with those types of linguistic signifiers. God is also not a being who resides above. Furthermore, He is not an inherent directorial force who set things into motion at some point only to allow human life (or nature) to unfold blindly. In addition, He is not Augustine's "is *is*" whose essence transcends human thought and discourse. In summation, Joseph Prabhu writes, "[Hegel] calls the 'bad infinite,' an infinite merely set over against the finite, and therefore external to or bounded by the finite."[174] So Hegel forecloses God's infinite nature through rational means perpetrated by human parameters constructed on earth or in the finite realm.

Further, Hegel's perspective of logic provides insight into his idea of God. He writes, "[Logic] is metaphysical theology [because it] treats the evolution of the idea of God in the ether of pure thought."[175] Hegel's "Logic" as the center of reality illustrates his rational viewpoint of reality itself. The use of logic brings God (and the world) into existence, rather than God existing *a priori* and creating the world *ex nihilo*. Being metaphysical in nature, Nietzsche correctly identifies Hegel's emphasis on logic as part of the progressive death of God through metaphysics.

If the consciousness of humans produces religion, then God exists as (or through) a historical process. J. A. Leighton summarizes, "The Hegelian *Logic* is . . . an attempt to trace the evolution in the conception of the ultimate fact, God."[176] This ultimate fact becomes "Absolute" through the development to a final category "known as God."[177] The dichotomous relationship of the subject / object complicates. As radical theologian Thomas Altizer notes, "The break between objectivity and subjectivity . . . is consummated in Christianity . . . [and is] the final ending of transcendent objectivity . . . [so] objectivity . . . [is] the realization of subjectivity . . . therefore objectivity perishes as objectivity . . . 'in-itself.'"[178] In other words, once the subject and object unite, supernatural objectivity dissipates through the unity with the subjective experience of mind and body, which conflates to objectivity within the paradoxical boundaries of subjective thought.

Therefore, the object cannot be a boundless object depicted by subjects, but rather the object resides within the subjective experience and manifests by the historical process of metaphysical relations. Richard Dien Winfield explains, "Hegel logically captures this process . . . in terms of the Idea, [which] unites concept and objectivity in and through themselves . . . The embodied mind . . . [exhibits] the truth of the Idea . . . where body and mind unite objectivity and subjectivity."[179] Simply put, the transcendent objectivity of God comes down to earth as an object of thought from human subjectivity. To Hegel, the incarnation of Christ also displays the objectivity of God on earth. Therefore, the object, God, unites with the subject, human, in rational thought. To emphasize, the historical process in which God manifests himself clearly buttresses Hegel's ideas on God. Darrel E. Christensen reiterates, "Where the dialectical history is under consideration . . . the emerging identity [of God] comprehends the most comprehensive opposites, being and thought, which identity is actuality."[180] The actual existence of God realizes itself in this way.

In addition, Hegel alters rationality to incorporate contradictions as reasonable. Philosopher Stephen Hicks explains that Kant was "too trapped in the old Aristotelian logic of non-contradiction"[181] and that Hegel formulated a "better kind of reason, one that embraces contradictions and sees the whole of reality as evolving out of contradictory forces."[182] The previously reviewed theologians as well as Descartes and Kant, employed reason to make God a universal (non-contradictory) and rationally cogent defined being, but Hegel admits to the contradictions embedded within God's nature. This assertion contributes to the death of God because the metaphysical God can no longer be successfully reasoned without accepting contradictions. This results in the further ascension of faith. And these contradictions illuminate the precariousness of the previously reviewed claims about the metaphysical God.

The examples of Descartes, Kant, and Hegel support Nietzsche's central claim of the murdered God. The complexity of reason that these philosophers utilized to keep God alive while they implicitly argued against long-standing conceptions of God, illustrates how "reason" first explains God, and then kills God. Nietzsche conceives this idea as the natural outcome that stems from the original concepts that surround the Christian God. In other words, when one proposes a figure that encompasses every possible positive attribute in the most perfect possible manifestation, then that figure will fail to meet those expectations in objective reality. Hicks clarifies when he writes, "[Christian] cosmology . . . posits a perfect being that generates evil, [and] believes in a just being that gives humans independent judgment [free will] but punishes them for using it."[183] Therefore, the omnipotent, omnipresent, omnibenevolent, and omniscient metaphysical God who gives humans the gift of free will and is laden with contradictions, dies. Nietzsche is able to claim the death of this God while he also forecasts a replacement that embodies the same principles as the murdered God. This new God is science, which later manifests as advanced technology.

Chapter 4

The Rise of the Technological God

Physicist Rustum Roy constructed the analogy that science is to technology as theology is to religion.[184] In this sense, the broad (significant) theoretical assertions come from science while the application of those assertions manifest in technology. Similarly, theology offers the framework for religions to operate. More importantly, the worlds of science and theology and technology and religion circulate near or around the others. To follow this analogy through, one detects that the way humans practice religion corresponds with the way humans practice technology. However, the phrase "practice technology" remains out of popular use. One does not practice technology, one uses technology. Does one use a religion? To use a religion one might pray, confess, or attend church. Still, the analogy seems to fail. But perhaps paradoxically it makes the issue clearer. Perhaps, we are practicing technology. To practice technology means to use it religiously. Each text message, search query, or interactive video session involves the practice of technology, the new religion.

Before a full discussion on technology as religion, the discussion on science as theology requires interrogation. The advent of science follows the pattern of rational metaphysics, which Nietzsche identifies. The Scholastic thinkers employed their extensive reasoning capabilities to explicate and promote, with as much exactitude as possible, the nature of God. Therefore, the method remained in place for Descartes, Kant, and Hegel to retain God, yet reason Him to death. For instance, Lacan claims that "Descartes inaugurates the initial bases of a science in which God has nothing to do."[185] Therefore, it is only appropriate that science uses its methods to create a God that does things, through advanced technology.

During this time, science develops its method with Galileo, Kepler, Bacon, Newton, and Descartes, all of whom were theists. In fact, Theologian Alan G. Padgett confirms that "There was no conflict in principle, between . . . science and religion before the enlightenment . . . [and] theology and religion were instrumental in the development of the empirical, mathematical rationality of modern science."[186] Thus, the later medieval and Renaissance periods generally maintain a healthy coexistence between science and theology. Padgett declares that the "Enlightenment prejudice against authority, tradition, and religious faith . . . [aimed] to destroy the political authority of the church in Europe."[187] The Enlightenment period signals the beginning of the major rift between science and theology. Again, though, reason applied to theology itself set this process in motion. Furthermore, the teleology of the two fields of thought continues. Science as theology starts with the mechanistic concept of the world. Mumford looks at the period of astronomical discoveries as the central time when the mechanistic scientific worldview becomes a new religion. He writes, "The period between Copernicus and Newton [contributed] a new outlook . . . while the Christian Heaven shrank, the astronomical heaven expanded . . . [which created] a profound religious reorientation . . . [that] accounts for the immense authority that the astronomical and mechanical world pictured exerted."[188]

Of course, the scientists never really challenge the authority of the church during this time. Even though the earth-centered universe proves implausible and alters the cosmos of the Church, the ultimate explanation of the new order still revolves around the magnificent order of God's creation (the cosmological argument). Mumford makes sure to note, "Despite conflicts and skirmishes with the Church, science produced no martyrs. Copernicus, Galileo, Kepler, and Descartes . . . discreetly sidestepped martyrdom"[189] even though Galileo ushers in the negative of subjective experience in favor of the complete and total understanding of the objective world.

This eliminates Nietzsche's Dionysian human experience from the scientific method. Mumford explains that Galileo's successors "pulverized . . . cultural heritage into that which was the measurable, public, 'objective,' repeatable . . . [and] obliterated the basic facts of human existence."[190] Moreover, "The new cult . . . promoted an immense concentration on the mastery of earthly life: exploration, invention, conquest, colonization, all centered on immediate fulfillment. Now, not the hereafter was what counted."[191] Consequently, the path to certainty and truth as it pertains to objective reality no longer resides in the spiritual realm where the human lives as a subjective and moral being. Rather, all subjectivity belongs to those who employ the scientific method to apprehend objective truth of human objects and everything else in the natural world on earth and in the universe. Cultural expressions of human existence (life after death, for example) lose their status in the universal mechanical framework, since subjectivity informs culture. This allows a one-dimensional viewpoint to usurp all other claims of certainty.

Nietzsche makes an important point concerning the futility and even the danger of the scientific society in *Thus Spoke Zarathustra* when a man lies in a swamp, covered by leeches, as he studies the workings of their brains.[192] Zarathustra confronts the scientist who says, "How long already have I pursued this one thing, the brain of the leech, so that the slippery truth no longer slips away from me here."[193] Nietzsche criticizes the over examination of every tiny aspect of nature and life on earth. However, this examination by the scientist does not remain benign. When the Apollonian overpowers the Dionysian, the rules of the mechanical hold sway in society. In a sense, the scientist who studies the brain of the leech asserts his will-to-power upon the leech. By analogy, the scientific viewpoint of the cosmos and the earth take power over the human mind and results in a singular outlook for humanity.

As the theology, through the Scholastics and the like, created a singular point of view of life mediated by God (and them), the scientific project replaces theology as the new dogma of mediation for the human subject (object). Babette Babich declares, "Our lives today, in whatever part of the world, for the rich and for the poor, are mediated more and more by technology. We take this 'connectedness' to be the 'gift' of science."[194] Mediation of subjects occurs through objects. Therefore, the object gives subjectivity. More alarmingly, perhaps, is the notion that the subjects lose subjectivity to the object and thus the roles reverse where the subject is the (technological object) and the subjects become human objects. Roy explains, "Contemporary science, which once was about a human's experience of nature, has retreated to the outer fringes of magnitude away from the interest or comprehension of ninety-five percent of humans."[195] Roy's point is accurate, but Nietzsche saw scientific specialization as occurring much earlier. Simply put, it has always been less than five percent of humans who have had interest or comprehension of the knowledge of science. Moreover, the same is true of theological specialization and the percentage of those who had comprehension or even access to it during the time of Augustine to Anselm.

Descartes lives as one of the main progenitors of the scientific project and, hence, epitomizes Nietzsche's central point in God's death and in the

Apollonian dominance of the future. In *Discourse on Method,* Descartes insists that "knowing the force and action of fire, water, air, the stars, the heavens, and all other bodies that surround us, we might also apply them in the same way to all the uses to which they are adapted, and thus render ourselves the lords and possessors of nature."[196] Descartes use of terms such as "the heavens" (as opposed to the sky or even the universe) and "lords of nature" to infer the relationship of the scientific project to the coming new theology of domination. The suggestion to apply the knowledge of the mechanistic properties of the natural world to "all uses" proves particularly unsettling because it implies the enforcement of an entire machine-like society. Mumford confirms, "Thus the ultimate aim of science, the proof of both its truth and its efficacy, would be to make all behavior as predictable as the movements of the heavenly bodies."[197] To support this idea further, Babich states, "Science increasingly defines what is real and dominates the globe in a singularly irresistible fashion."[198]

Science begins to set up a teleological and utopian scenario of progress from its method and application, which replaces the Christian concept of heaven. Heidegger explains this aptly as he writes, "The flight from the world into the suprasensory is replaced by historical progress. The otherworldly goal of everlasting bliss is transformed into the earthly happiness of the greatest number. The engineering of life on earth will produce happiness and contentment."[199] In addition, the early work of

Mumford proposes utopian city planning, but he later altered his perspective. Christopher May affirms, "[Mumford's] pre-40s work on cities and planning . . . exhibited a preference for technocratic, centralized bureaucratic control. However, by the 1960s, when his interest had turned almost exclusively to the problem of technology, he rejects sorts of Utopian visions which had influence him in the pre-war period, seeing them as essentially totalitarian."[200] Nietzsche calls it "The delusion of limitless power."[201] In context, Nietzsche speaks of a Socratic quest for objective knowledge while neglecting the subjective experiences of music and art (distinct cultural expressions outside of the objective). Nietzsche rejects objectivism and stands in opposition to a purely objective standpoint divorced from our subjective involvement in the world.[202]

Gregory Morgan Swer reinforces this by claiming that "The gain in scientific knowledge and predictive power was offset by a corresponding loss in knowledge of the subjective, qualitative dimensions of existence."[203] These subjective dimensions could only be manifest in utilitarian routines mechanized by the universal production of necessities scientifically calibrated for the utmost efficiency. Commenting on utopian literature (*City of the Sun, New Atlantis,* and *Christianoplis*), Frank Manuel mentions, "The scientist was differentiated from other men of learning and began to play the dominant role in the imaginary society. The role of the scientist and the institutions of science in these three works set important form-giving patterns for many later scientific establishments."[204] In essence, the imaginary society exists as the ultimate expression of human organization through a sculpted configuration model that eventually becomes the governing paradigm. However, unlike the utopias of the literature, the manifestation of the model proves problematic as this model "repressed humanity and destroyed the environment."[205] When one traces the movement from the metaphysical assertion of God and the all-encompassing theology, of which it conforms to the method of science as a means to inform human enterprise and engagement, it is obvious that Rustum Roy's comparison of science as theology appears valid.

Technology as religion serves as the other side of Roy's analogy. Larry Stapleton, Senior Academic at the Waterford Institute of Technology, uses the term "technoculture."[206] He means, "The interpenetration of the human world to the machine world through which human existence is to be mediated and shaped."[207] It is significant to note that the language used for describing science in the world shares the vocabulary and usage with the terms that describe technology. For example, one might say, "The human is overpowered by scientific analysis or the human is overpowered by technological advancement." Any discussion on the nature of the Christian theological God demonstrates the mediation of human life through the prevailing religious dogma of the period. Despite the manifestation of human ingenuity in the form of newly constructed technology (the printing press, for example), the great majority of people found their lives mediated through religious practice and power. Since the Church ruled and God was absolutely perfect, mediation could be through nothing else. Consequently, the religious culture (religioculture) is the technoculture. Mediation bears significant relevance in understanding the power of technology in human life. Ultimately, if scientific knowledge exhibits a privileging of the mechanical in the operation of nature, then technology stands as the application of the mechanical operations of scientific discovery.

Science sees the machines in the universe and engineers fabricate the corresponding artificial machines artificially. Mumford declares, "In a world of machines, or of creatures that can be reduced to machines, technocrats would indeed be gods."[208] This claim provides a fine analogy, but rather than gods, the technocrats (scientists and engineers) live as the Augustines and Anselms (theologians) of times past. Stapleton refers to these technocrats as "functional rationalists."[209] He writes, "Functional rationalism is obsessed with the integration in which knowledge and insight is not embodied in humans but codified into data processing machines."[210] When the human reduces to a machine, the machine becomes a mode of human expression, of which the mediation to nature becomes empty and the connection to other humans (machines) becomes a mediated relation between mechanical objects. The codes in machines dictate behavior of the human subject. Since technocrats or functional rationalists build these codes, they mediate the connections to humanity to the without and the within. Roy explains, "Technology functions to replace what traditional religions offer."[211] The religious experience alters how human subjects mediate with the suprasensory. This religious experience becomes a technological experience.

Thus, the qualities of the suprasensory must remain inside the codified expressions of mediation. Otherwise, the nature of belief becomes demystified. In other words, if Roy's figures on the percentage of those whose interest and comprehension of applied science reversed (95% of people understand and care about how technologies actually function), the system would implode. In order for it to be religious, like during the time of the Scholastics, the technocrats must keep the mystery of the object in place. Consequently, science and engineering (applied science) cannot actually fulfill its unrealistic assertion that it is a disinterested method for understanding. Roy confirms, "Basic science, the kind that is determined by the curiosity of individual investigators alone, not aimed at any goal or product but at understanding is coming to an end."[212] Over one hundred years earlier, Nietzsche already penned Roy's claim about science. Nonetheless, its accuracy illustrates the role of the functional rationalist as the new theologians who support and propagate religion as technology. Mumford recognizes that "the immediate outcome of the new [scientific] system of thought and de-emotionalized statements was temporarily a happy one, for it cooled off the overheated atmosphere of theological controversy left over from the Reformation and the Counter Reformation . . . but the ultimate result of this mechanistic doctrine was to raise the machine to a higher status than any organism or at best to admit grudgingly that higher organisms were supermachines."[213]

Finally, the tie to science and technology bears the dictates of faith. Nietzsche discusses the element of faith. Avron Kulak summarizes "Because the unconditional will to truth, which the natural sciences presuppose in order to begin, for Nietzsche, equally religious and secular, the secular is, it turns out, the truth of the religious, but only because the religious is equally the truth of the secular."[214] This "will to truth" constitutes the same act of faith found within the Scholastic metaphysical realm and also within Descartes, Kant, and Hegel. Nietzsche offers a clear explanation, "It is still a metaphysical faith upon which our faith in science rests, that even we seekers of knowledge today, we godless anti-metaphysicians still take our fire, too from the flame lit by faith that is thousands of years old, that Christian faith . . . that God is truth, that truth is divine."[215] Finally, Nietzsche makes the profound connection extremely evident when he writes, "The good faith in science, the prejudice in its favor that dominates the modern state and formerly dominated even the church."[216] This establishes the transitional period from the church through Nietzsche to our contemporary moment where science and technology rules every practice through its dominance in daily human life.

Moreover, Willem Drees provides the most apt explanation for our times. He claims, "We look to the engineers for our salvation. This is not to be seen as an antireligious move, as we may appreciate their knowledge and skills as gifts of God, as possibilities to serve the neighbor."[217] The overt intermingling of faith based dictums and the technicians of the global scientific empire infer the imminent new system of technological religious conceptions. Drees, who welcomes the complete transformation of faith, further claims, "Faith in technological culture is not that different from what it has been, because we humans are not that different. We are still vulnerable [confirming Freud], still looking for orientation, for something to hold on to, for a song that strengthens us."[218] While Nietzsche foresaw the separation of the Apollonian and the Dionysian, Drees employs the metaphor of the song with the advancement of technological faith in objects. The current consensus among proponents of the global proliferation of gadgets, mix metaphors to produce the connection between creative artistic creations based in subjective human enterprise with the objectivity technology implants in the human experience.

Drees does not mention a key element of Nietzsche's fears. Mark E. Warren notes, "For Nietzsche . . . all ideas concerning universal laws and necessities, truths, and values mask their particular and interested relations to modes of power."[219] Drees metaphor serves as a narrow disingenuous attempt to connect humanity through a shared sentimentality to the finality of organization and security. His statement is the mask that Nietzsche discusses. It blocks from view the underlying power of the technological theology and priesthood. At one time, hope for a positive scientific future existed. Virgilio Aquino Rivas describes, "Men who possessed of honorable intentions . . . alert mankind that a new religion, that of technocracy, was emerging. Unfortunately, [these men had] dark sinister intentions."[220] In addition, he declares, "God had returned to earth, but under a new cloak . . . so expansive that it threatened to conquer the planet . . . in other words, the annihilation of the whole planet."[221] Nietzsche fears nihilism. Those like Mumford, who are critical of the religiosity of technological advancement, fear global catastrophe. Incidentally, Erling Hope feels that "technology becomes invisible, unnoticed, its interface becomes intuitive and gestural rather than technical. It becomes the medium in which we live and move and have our being."[222] Hope suggests a reality where the awareness of technology becomes obsolete, similar to how the awareness of the natural world has become obsolete. With his thesis, we look to Augustine's "God is *is*,"[223] of which God simply defies our conceptual abilities and becomes everything to the point of Hegelian negation. Despite the overwhelming supremacy of science as theology and technology as religion, God remains unidentified. To comprehend the intersection of Hope's thesis with Augustine's God, we can ask: what scientific and technological entity defies humanity and becomes invisible in Augustinian terms? Google. Therefore, if "God is *is*" then Google is *is*, and, likewise, Google is God because God is God.

Chapter 5

Google: A Technological God

"Google's techno-utopian vision and earthly appetite for power rest on the foundational Enlightenment belief in progress"[224]

All Human Activity: Mediated and Informed by Google

Google's origins overtly illustrate a mode of operation (and motivation) outside of profit driven consumerism. Essentially, this moves Google beyond the simple construction of a multinational corporation bent on making money. Although James Walters, in his book *Baudrillard and Theology*, notes, "[Baudrillard's] formulation of the advanced capitalist predicament is also reminiscent of Michel Foucault's 'biopower' in the way in which, through consumerism, capitalist processes have pervaded all aspects of everyday life and thought"[225] Walker ties Baudrillard to Foucault as it relates to the singular momentary actions that contribute to the vast mediation of productive / consumptive power in basic daily movements. But the thesis of capitalist consumerism as a means to dictate or mediate all aspects of life no longer fully resolves the question of technological omni-prevalence. Google's (potential / eventual / inevitable) global omnipresence or total mediation of human function, as Foucault's "biopower" and Baudrillard's "inertial mass," fails because the processes that pervade all aspects of everyday life and thought, while firmly embedded in consumerism, ascend to a state where consumerism becomes irrelevant and, more importantly, *unconscious* in the masses' use of (Google's) technological interfaces. In parallel, although the church(es), held to financial aims in terms of God (God needs this money), which maneuvered the daily life of its parishioners, God encompassed a more highly evolved or intrinsically transcendent purpose. Taken with Augustine's "God is *is*" (Google is *is*), the rationale of total pervasion through centrally economic means dissolves as an aggregate explanation.

Furthermore, the origination of God, both the pre-Mosaic Law or Pre-Nicaean Creed, implies a supra-presence that invades motivational precepts while it interacts with normalizing constructs throughout the central survival navigation in human movement. In Lacanian terms (through Freud), the unconscious presupposes "the submission to the father by creating a FatherGod."[226] To be more precise, German Psychotherapist Jürgen Braungardt accurately accounts that the truth of religion (God) "exists in the unconscious as a repressed memory and manifests itself in repetition."[227] The repetition involves a manifested construction both from above and below in Foucault's power relations and Baudrillard's inertial masses. Therefore, Google acts as a representation of unconscious drives that aim for the desire of the ideal ego in materiality that composes a naturalized system of material movement or creation of the ideal ego. Each Google search enacts a reinforcement of the domination of technic narrowing, individual physical automation, and psycho-physical worship. Lacan offers the undercurrent of power over the body so prominent in religious dogma when he asks, "Do we not see . . . the emergence of that which forced Freud to find in the myths of the death of the father the regulation of desire?"[228] Thus, death and desire work in relation to conceptualizing Lacan's version of God, and within the context of technological or applied science as an extension or usurper of the metaphysical God, the death of Nietzsche's God admits to the desire of the very "biopower" embedded in Google's structure.

In terms of regulation, which surfaces when deconstructed through Foucault, Google aims for the desire at the initial presence of the initial creation of the search and fortifies the desire when search becomes a regulatory practice. For instance, Harvard Psychologist and Journalist Robert Epstein reports that "Google's ubiquitous search engine has indeed become the gateway to virtually all information, handling 90 percent of search in most countries."[229] Therefore, Google fully articulates omniscience through regulatory practice, with desire at its base. This establishes that Google virtually controls all search. With this control, conceptualizing the normalization through religious dogma becomes an appropriate extrapolation through basic Lacanian discourse. The maintenance of such power previously required an interlocutor or, more appropriately, a mediator (speaker) whose presence dictated a naturalizing process. Lacan, through Freud cites the doctor as the mediator of which desire and prohibition manifest through language.[230] In religious terms, the mediator comprises the class of priests, whether in the process of preaching, confession, or otherwise. The clergy always includes a visible material relation who offers, at least in practical terms, a two-way discourse to the individual (of the inertial masses). Google search eliminates the physical mediator regardless of the multiple technicians who oversee the operation of the technics.

In more cynical terms, the mediator manifests physically in the plastic form of the screen and communicatively in the virtual form of the autocomplete and the list of results. This places desire into an automated (or regulated) (pseudo)confessional space. Beyond information and beyond any degree of specifically locatable rationality, desire initiates through the unrecognizable register of the Imaginary. Lacan mentions the relationship between analyst and analysand (Google search and human searching) when he notes, "Something is mystically placed here on the person who listens to him."[231] The implication of analyst as God (Father) persists, but complicates in the narcissistic moment when the analysand puts himself "in the place of his interlocutor."[232] Here, the physical nature of the analyst dissipates, and the analysand takes on the God syndrome. The question arises: what mediator (dis)appears when the screen replaces the physical? A more fully cynical answer consists of the complete disappearance of the human mediator, but revives less cynically with the insertion of God. Moreover, the representatives of God (clergy and analyst) always fulfill the formerly necessary role condensed in the (human) physical. With the screen, these mediators disappear while the material presence of the screen results in a hyperreal manifestation of supreme regulatory mediation.

The consequences of this alteration involves the shift in the Imaginary and the Symbolic orders. Since the Imaginary contains the bed-place of ideal ego and unconscious narcissism,[233] it serves as a location to graft resistance to regulatory dictation. How can this continue to operate if the symbolic function of the Father becomes mediated through the virtual? Delay summarizes Lacan's symbolic (Father) as "everything collected in our psyche from our experience. It is our parents and friendships, our social norms and taboos, our gods and demons."[234] Within a hegemonic Google search, a dual regulatory machine deflates the symbolic further than the Christian God and its clergy, *before* the death of God. The screen as medium regulates the senses in McLuhan terms while the content regulates through calculated results.

First, to address McLuhan and the senses, he writes, "The effects of technology . . . alter sense ratios or patterns of perception steadily and without any resistance."[235] The advent of the screen offers a sensory dimension that differs in experience from the one mediated in two-way human communication. McLuhan's key phrase, "patterns of perception," exemplifies the sensory engagement with the screen that encompass the ideas of Foucault and Baudrillard. From the vantage point of perception, McLuhan relates the myth of Narcissus to illustrate the ratio of sense to "numbness."[236] The screen numbs. McLuhan continues, "This extension of himself [Narcissus] by mirror numbed his perceptions until he became the servomechanism of his own extended or repeated image."[237] French Author Jean Querzola refers to this numbness as "electronic narcosis."[238] He continues, "The computer prosthesis . . . provides us with a . . . bio-electronic mirror, in which each person, like some digital Narcissus, will slide along the trajectory of a death drive and sink in his or her own image."[239] The biological element involves the sense ratio inherent in the immediate interaction between the human and the screen. Highly acclaimed writer Nicholas Carr provides the evidence for McLuhan and Querzola's claim through neuroscience. He concludes:

> The recent discoveries about neuroplasticity make the essence of the intellect more visible, its steps and boundaries easier to mark. They tell us that the tools man has used to support or extend his nervous system, all those technologies that through history have influenced how we find, store, and interpret information, how we direct our attention and *engage our senses* . . . have shaped the physical

> structure and workings of the human mind. Their use has strengthened some neural circuits and weakened others, reinforced certain mental traits while leaving others to fade away."[240]

Therefore, the vital questions are: what senses does Narcissus employ when he sees his reflection in the river, and what senses do humans employ when looking in the smart screen? In the monologue of search, Google reflects an image unrecognizable to the human object, or at least an unrecognized version of the self. This vision ignites the Imaginary register, the ideal ego, of Lacan's Names of the Father.

Since Lacan's register of the Imaginary is the "domain of narcissism,"[241] and the Imaginary, according to Lacan is what is "artificially reproduced,"[242] the human object "sinks" into a state of narcosis or narcissistic fixation. To explain, Freud states, "The ideal ego answers to everything that is expected of the higher nature of man. As a substitute for a longing for the father, it contains the germ from which all religions have evolved."[243] The ideal ego rests at the foundation of the God creation and also results in a continuous aim to fulfill this ideal through the death drive toward unquenchable desire. Lacan's "mirror stage" echoes Freud's assessment and, moreover, facilitates the endeavor of the human psyche to overcome the mystery of the image through the creation of the smart screen and the Google search. The search enacts this ideal driven performativity. Delay explains, "In the same way that one might look in a mirror and see an image more attractive than the image actually reflected, narcissism is unsatisfied with the conscious recognition of itself and compensates by creating a narrative . . . an Imaginary beyond the Imaginary."[244] Therefore, Lacan's Imaginary houses the birth of God (*ex nihilo* / beyond the Imaginary) and later the advent of (applied) science (the extension of God). Both require a narrative built within the psyche and both are epitomized in Google as a sensorial stalemate.

The narrative structure exemplifies the elaborate, colorful, and creative use of reason (and literary devices) found in Scholastic texts. This presents an ambiguity of the idea that "Man (is) God" and since "God is Dead," so is "Man." The concept of God, when taken to its psychoanalytical limit, reveals to the human that God was the Ideal human, all along; and lives as the ultimate and absolutely singular simulacra of the Imaginary register. The over four thousand pages of narrative from Thomas stands in alignment with the complex programing language of the computer. The theological narrative turns into an unspecified story void of linearity, conflict, spirit, or emotion. The only result manifests on the screen and bears witness to an unknowable author (programmer). Programming language which indicates the (anti)presence of pure simulacra only reveals the emptiness of historical human linguistic signifiers.

Baudrillard describes this situation by analyzing a chess match between Kasparov, a human, and a computer program named Deep Blue. The human wins the chess match. Baudrillard writes:

> But, to come back to Kasparov, if he won, it was surely because he is (metaphorically) capable of speaking more than one language: that of the emotions, of intuition, of the stratagem, in a word, the language of play [Dionysian], not to mention the language of calculation. Whereas Deep Blue speaks only the language of calculation [Apollonian]. The day this latter language prevails, in whatever form, Kasparov will be beaten. The day man himself speaks only that single language, the language of computers, he will be beaten.[245]

To explain, a global speak of religious rationale as exemplified in *Summa Theologica* offers a global simulation of language usage. It represents a closed system of homogeneity or as Baudrillard might say a fabrication of "non-communication."[246] Nonetheless, Thomas's lengthy text carries notions of genuine emotive narration with clear and identifiable linguistic signifiers. This keeps language within the realm of humanity while maintaining the ideal ego of God. The language of calculation manifests without these human elements and transcends human considerations. The only consideration is calculation. In Lacanian terms, the computer language incorporates the ideal ego into the overlapping register of the Symbolic.

Lacan notes that the "Symbolic is the presence expressed in absence."[247] Therefore, the Imaginary is the conscious while the Symbolic is the unconscious. Eventually, Lacan's Real reveals itself. Delay explains, "The Symbolic is an intermediate register of sorts, the filter which the Real enters and becomes interpreted for the Imaginary." So, the *Summa Theologica* offers the Real of God the Father in the conscious real through an elaborate rationale motivated by an ideal ego understood in narcissistic consciousness. But the Symbolic unconscious motivation insists on the creation of the ideal ego. Furthermore, in psychoanalysis, "conscious justification [such as *Summa Theologica*] for a viewpoint is always of secondary importance."[248] The language of calculation manifests or simulates the Real on a smart screen with a singular homogenous vantage point. How does one grasp the unconscious in a computer programming language of calculation?

To repeat Baudrillard, "The day man himself speaks only that single language, the language of computers, he will be beaten."[249] Querzola notes that the "development of . . . information technology is accompanied by the dissolution of the personality structure we call Oedipal."[250] This makes Lacan's Symbolic register one dimensional and implodes all human constructed regulations, laws, and (cultural) mores into one single module of calculation.

In essence, Google search contains the properties which perpetually reenact and decode all the psychological modes of desire characterized by modes of worship. It delimits the sensory data and shifts potential analysis to what McLuhan describes as "pattern recognition"[251] both inside and outside of the smart screen. It also transcends the simple and ineffective explanation from a strictly economic analysis. To elaborate, "Google is search's most powerful innovator and driver. From its late 1990s inception, the algorithm PageRank™, which underpins Google's search technologies, transformed the practice and conceptualization of what it was to search the Web."[252] The algorithm demotes the role of the Symbolic from the human and promotes the artificial unconscious of computer language of calculation.

Of course, Baudrillard's hyperbolic anxiety rests upon the human becoming the machine and, thus, eliminating the human. With the global dominance of Google, algorithm becomes, in Foucault's terms, normalized. Hillis et. al. explain, "Online and mobile search practices and the algorithms that determine results are accepted by most searchers as utilitarian, though widely understood to be powerful, their very ubiquity has quickly naturalized them into the backgrounds, fabrics, spaces, and places of everyday life."[253] Hillis et. al use the term "naturalize," but a more fitting term might be artificialize. Therefore, the more naturalized Google's algorithms become in human life, the more artificially constructed human life becomes. This is the technological God at work. Regardless, the central point involves the constant mediation of Google search embedded in human existence.

Google is God

While humans previously saw the metaphysical God as the mediator of all interaction and activity that mediator is now the technological God. The scientific ideal ego. Ken Auletta, author of *Googled: The End of the World as we Know It*, describes the creators of this mediation when he writes, "Google's leaders are not cold businessmen; they are cold engineers. They are scientists, always seeking new answers. They seek a construct, a formula, an algorithm that both graphs and predicts behavior. They naively believe that most mysteries, including the mysteries of human behavior, are unlocked with data."[254] To turn to Foucault, the dual relationship between the creator and the rank and file participant reinforces the omnipotence (and omniscience) of Google. While the engineers, who aim to dehumanize the globe, construct systems to unlock the "mysteries of human behavior," they actually inform, construct, or dictate the human behavior, itself. Foucault already discusses this system of calculation by the Panopticon. He writes:

> The Panopticon should be the formula for the whole of government[.] . . . It must give way to everything due to natural mechanisms in . . . behavior[.] . . . It must give way to these mechanisms and make no other intervention . . . [except] . . . supervision. Government . . . is only to intervene when it sees that something is not happening according to the general mechanics of behavior.[255]

Google is God

Although Foucault speaks of government, Google carries more wealth and power than traditional statist governments.[256] Essentially, Google attempts to catalogue and analyze "natural" human behavior without direct intervention, and create "search" based on the data. It only intervenes when human behavior conflicts with the data. The intervention includes a shift in the algorithms, which alters "natural" human behavior.[257] The language of calculation solidifies the Symbolic regulation of the ideal ego while it prescribes the models of normalcy (or what is natural) for human behavior.

In this system, humans no longer need Protestant Theologian Johnathan Edwards'[258] hellfire to behave accordingly for God; they simply participate in a calculated system of Google constructed algorithms. Power from top to bottom reinforced from bottom to top.

Google engineers overlook McLuhan's basic thesis that "the medium is the message." Human behavior cannot be a mystery when the medium, through which the behavior of the human is manifest, carries inherent outcomes of human behavior. The simple existence of the smart screen communicates certain behaviors by design. Therefore, human behavior *is* by design. Google guarantees specific human behavior because it owns the medium. Since it handles "90% of search in most countries,"[259] the human mind can be molded through the use of Google search until all life is basic simulation. For example, Foucault mentions, "Throughout the penal procedure and the implementation of the sentence there swarms a whole series of subsidiary authorities."[260] Obviously, the use of Google search is not an exercise of governmental legal punishment, but there is a major element of control over the body and mind of the individual within Google search. The main point lies in the "series of subsidiary authorities." In basic terms, when ninety percent of people utilize a single informational medium, this "swarm" shares behavioral attitudes, ideas, movement, and preferences. Eventually, without any thought, the swarm "naturally" behaves by the dictates of the algorithm (and the medium) or as "subsidiary authorities." This is microphysics of power and the manifestation of Baudrillard's inertial masses. This is omnipotence.

The Omnipotence of Google

Omnipotence involves the power to create. In terms of Google, former Google CEO, Eric Schmidt said, "Our goal is to change the world."[261] The idea of change, Schmidt implies, relates to the idea of eternal scientific progress. This began through the advent of reason that Scholastic theologians employed through Descartes and Bacon's scientific method to the proclamation of the death of the metaphysical God by Nietzsche and the rise of science as the authority for apprehending the world. Google's changing of the world can be logically interpreted as the omnipotent creation of a new world. Baudrillard's famous interpretation of the Borges fable, in which the map of the territory covers the territory, offers one evident reference to this change. He writes, "The territory no longer precedes the map, nor does it survive it. It is nevertheless the map that precedes the territory."[262] Foucault supplies another obvious reference with the construction Bentham's Panopticon. He states, "The Panopticon is a machine."[263] Therefore, the architectural / mechanical construction allows for only predetermined activity, a specifically determined state of being, and a prescribed range of sensory input.

It is significant to note that God as a human creation aligns with Google as a human creation. The former as the creator of the universe, as proposed by theologians and the latter in the realm of the contemporary God of science and technology through, literally, Sergei Brin and Larry Page. Both constitute human creations (*ex nihilio*) and both exit the axis of something with direct entry and sublime clarity into something that is Real in the Lacanian sense of the term. Moreover, the Scholastics' God became complicated over time and became a being whose explanation rationally eliminated the being, itself. Moreover, the Real was overwhelmed by the intersection of the Imaginary and the Symbolic, in other words, by meaning.

The Christian God created the human in His own image, and "The goodness of God is reflected in [human] creation."[264] If God created it, it is good. Thomas replies to the objection that "God can do evil things if He will"[265] by replying, "Both the antecedent and consequent are impossible: as if one were to say: If man is an ass he has four feet."[266] Google creates (the human) in its own image. Google's motto is "Don't Be Evil." If Google creates it, it is not evil.[267] To return to Google search, discussed briefly, it functions as a reflective *and* two-way mirror, of which the human gaze returns upon itself. In this sense, Google's original search enterprise epitomizes the grandiose nature and goodness of its creation.

God's ability to create involves establishing the "laws of the heavens and the earth." Of course, ample scriptural evidence supports the theologians' assertions which relate to the laws of the universe as set by God. For instance, Job 38:32-33 states, "Can you lead forth a constellation in its season, and guide the Bear with her satellites? Do you know the ordinances of the heavens, or fix their rule over the earth?" (*New International Version*). Also, Jeremiah 31:25 notes, "This is what the LORD says, he who appoints the sun to shine by day, who decrees the moon and stars to shine by night, who stirs up the sea so that its waves roar, the LORD Almighty is his name" (*New International Version*). Essentially, the power of creation includes the parameters and rules for the objects within creation, and these are inherently good and for the good of His creation. Augustine refers to this as "eternal law." He mentions that "It is the law according to which it is just that all things be perfectly ordered," and "command that the soul be ruled by reason."[268] So,

God's power to create includes the rational elements of the cosmos. So does Google's.

Google search serves as the beacon of creation on the internet and lives as a testament to rationality beyond the grasp of its human followers / users. It constantly indexes and organizes the web through rational methods by employing algorithms. For example, in their nine-year longitudinal study, Dutch Professors Antal van der Bosch, Toine Bogers, and Maurice de Kunder report that Google indexed more than 45.7 billion pages by January, 2015.[269] Carr also describes Google's search methodology:

> A set of secret algorithms analyzes all the pages to create a comprehensive index of the Web, with every page ranked according to its relevance to particular keywords. The index is then replicated in each cluster. When a person enters a keyword into Google's search engine, the software routes the search to one of the clusters, where it is reviewed simultaneously by hundreds or thousands of servers.[270]

The mysterious nature of the algorithms coincides with the inability to confirm God's grand creation of the universe. The role of the individual to enter words into the search engine contributes to the power of Google's creation by obeying the eternal law of search. In Lacanian terminology, the keyword enters the Imaginary register where the Symbolic order of the "word" magnifies the center-point of the Real and circulates around its effective answers.

Identifying the most prominent (useful) webpage is an engineered moment of free will. While there are no wrong answers to the question of what page to choose, one's answer will determine the fate of future search results. Basically, search algorithm represents an attempt at organizing or computing the Symbolic chain of signifiers into a totalizing rational order, which means accessing the Real. The fact that the computation never stops illustrates the profound difficulty in accessing the Real through Symbolic and Imaginary realms of human subjectivity.

Regardless, the creation of the algorithm begins with the Word. In elementary terms, the desire always exists. Google's search engine requires the signifier as an attempt to access this inaccessible data. Even with the result of signifying chains, total access to the Lacanian Real remains impossible. Auletta explains, "They seek a construct, a formula, an algorithm that both graphs and predicts behavior. They naively believe that most mysteries, including the mysteries of human behavior, are unlocked with data."[271] While the algorithm is not God, the creator of the algorithm, Google is God. Just as the Scholastic theologians frame and shape the nature and essence of God, Google itself is the result of framing and sculpting through rational means. Thomas, for instance, employs reason to compose immense texts (*Summa Theologica*, etc.) that explain and represent God and humanity in relation to God, the rational (mathematical / engineered) based software and technological objects represent an explanation and representation of Google through human language.

Laws of the search redouble the co-paradoxical function of itself. Hillis et. al. explain, "Its models of a good search engine, a good search result, and good algorithmic logic have become normalized . . . because of its consecrated status, Google rules, and, as such, the rules set by the ruler define the parameters of the culture of search."[272] Again, the establishment of law comes from the human word or signifiers, but in the background of these established rules lives the specter of the Real. In the theologians' case, it is the Christian God. In the case of search, it is Google.

Basically, God's eternal law or Google's rules attain normalcy status and embed into the Symbolic realm of human subjectivity, and thus underpin the signifying order of the word. To repeat, Delay summarizes Lacan's symbolic (Father) as "everything collected in our psyche from our experience. It is our parents and friendships, our social norms and taboos, our gods and demons."[273] Therefore, any chain of signifiers established / normalized as law manifest predictably without necessary or immediate enforcement. Literal enforcement (policing) of the law only enters when the Imaginary realm of human subjectivity overpowers Symbolic prohibitions, such as those in the latent oedipal complex.

Since Google strives to never do evil, its human representatives attempt to evaluate the goodness of certain search data for a greater good or a "higher cause." Recall that Thomas notes that, "Those things which it belongs to God alone to do immediately, as, for example, to create . . . are said to be possible in reference to a higher cause."[274] Google also works upon the rationale of the higher cause. For instance, "In May 2016, Google blacklisted an entire industry, companies providing high-interest 'payday' loans . . . [it also] allowed Canadian drug companies to sell drugs illegally in the U.S. for years through the AdWords system."[275] Payday loans and overpriced American pharmaceuticals are wrapped up in immoral or unethical business practices. Therefore, Google's law represents a higher law of the good. One may object, as Epstein does, that Google is a "major investor in Lendup,"[276] which is in the payday loan business and, thus, is hypocritical.

But like the metaphysical God, if Google does it, it is good, and it is good because Google does it. Thomas (and the rest) offer the same defense for the goodness through creation (action) for God when he writes, "For God allows evils to happen in order to bring a greater good therefrom."[277] Even in the case of hellfire as Shadia Drury notes, "Augustine . . . takes it for granted that witnessing the torments of hell is integral to the pleasures of heaven."[278] Obviously, what appears as moral contradictions, in the mind of most humans, is easily rationalized by the very nature of God's goodness. And more obvious is that this applies to the essence of Google.

This correlates to Google's contemporary obsession with technological advancement that "draws on Enlightenment ideals of empiricism and its connection to ideals of progress,"[279] and requires moral hypocrisy for the sake of a utopian future. Hence, rationality easily clarifies what appears as hypocritical. In the case of Google, an entire campaign (and legal defense) of apologetics informs their Google Books Library Project, a project where Google aims to scan every book ever written into a central database (Hillis et. al. 146). The Project resulted in multiple copyright lawsuits.[280] Google's official statement reads, "The Library Project's aim is simple: make it easier for people to find relevant books."[281] The higher law of the good overshadows the inferior law of copyright. God's eternal law always overrides human temporal law.

Hegel's perspective proves valuable in order to comprehend the appearance of hypocrisy or contradictions in the nature of God and the technological God, Google. For instance, J. A. Leighton writes, "His highest philosophical achievement consists in his insight into the apparent contradictions of life. He sees clearly that we must hold conflicting views on ultimate questions without denying either view."[282] Stephen R. C. Hicks elaborates on Hegel's ideas: "The thrust of Enlightenment theology had been to alter religion by eliminating its contradictory theses in order to make it compatible with reason. Hegel's strategy is to accept that Judeo-Christian cosmology is rife with contradictions, but to alter reason in order to make it compatible with contradiction."[283] Although Hegel certainly influences major thinkers who still hold power in philosophical circles, the Enlightenment theology of eliminating contradiction also holds power. Nevertheless, just as "Judeo-Christian cosmology is rife with contradictions," so is the "cosmology" of applied science / advanced technology. Therefore, condemning embedded contradictions with Google's practices (e.g. "Don't Be Evil") appears a fruitless exercise, just as fruitless as rationalizing "God is Love" with eternal damnation in a fiery hell. In other words, referencing the contradictions of God's character only serves to reinforce God's character as one of contradiction.

Henceforth, the omnipotence found in the creation always reflects the good because the evil can only be good. Gmail, for instance, stands as one of Google's greatest creations. On April 1, 2004, Gmail became available for use. Author of *The Google Story* David Vise relates, "To blow the competition away and add a Google 'wow' factor . . . [and] to make the new service an instant hit, they planned to give away one free gigabyte of storage (1,000 megabytes) on Google's own computer network with each Gmail account."[284] He continues "One gigabyte was such an amazing amount of storage that Google told Gmail users they would never have to delete another email . . . [and] computer users would be able to find emails instantly . . . [because] Gmail search would be fast, accurate, and as easy to perform as a Google search."[285] The size of storage and the ability to search emails instantly provides the masses with the highest level of email technology.

The goodness of this creation appears universal and useful to the masses. Here, the use of the term "masses" refers to a very specific definition and application of the word as theorized by Baudrillard in his book, *In the Shadow of the Silent*

Majorities. He interprets this term as an "object." In other words, the masses as one single object.[286] This implies a homogenized singular object without individual or even group subjectivity.

Basically, Gmail offers fantastic email service, the best in the world according to reputable sources such as technorms.com, pcadvisor.co.uk, and pcmag.com. Interestingly, Geeksquad ranks Gmail at number one, while listing two major cons of the service.[287] They include: 1) Scans your email for keywords to target ads and 2) Ties you into Google's ecosystem. To address the first con, under the "Privacy Policy" for the use of Gmail, the masses must agree to the scanning of all their emails.[288] This concerned critics from the beginning. After all, since the metaphysical God is dead, the fear of the spirit in the sky who sees and knows everything is replaced by its technological equivalent. In fact, because of the massive storage space, "the first version of Gmail did not include a delete button."[289] The omission of the delete button highlights the illusion of the delete function, which formerly appeared to the masses as a way to permanently eliminate something from existence. Only through the removal of the delete option did the masses understand that an email (or any document, post, etc.), even if deleted, still lives on in a database. Auletta resumes, "This had an unforeseen effect: Users feared that Google would peek at e-mails. And Paul Buchheit's email scanning software . . . only fanned this fear . . . Critics said it was an invasion of privacy, that Big Brother was watching everything."[290] Gmail proves to not only be an essential element of Google's omnipotence through its creation for the good but also for its total omniscience. Ironically, Google employee number 23, Paul Buchheit, coined the phrase, "Don't Be Evil" while developing Google's email scanning (surveillance) software for use with AdSense.[291]

To address Geeksquad's second con, Gmail ties the masses into Google's ecosystem. Google creates entire suites of software and interfaces that illustrate its supreme power to create. For instance, Google offers its Apps for Education absolutely free to any institution who desires the service. Google touts that fifty million of the object mass uses "Google Apps for Education," while ten million use Google Classroom, and seven of eight Ivy League schools use Apps for Ed.

These apps include "Productivity Tools" such as Gmail, Drive, Docs, and Sheets. Google Drive, for example, provides unlimited personal storage through any participating educational institution. In basic terms, one can upload everything to Drive and provide links to all of the data. This gives professors and students the option to share any information they want to share, quickly and easily.

The best part is that all of these services are free! This is reminiscent of the Church's use of offering charity in the form of free food or shelter and, in return, virtually require the recipients to convert to the religion of the church. Journalist for *Consumerist*, Laura Northrup writes, "Many schools have migrated to using Google Apps for Education, which provides mail and a suite of other Google services to educators and students for free."[292] Obviously, these apps embody the creative power of Google and, more obviously, with the education of our children, for the good. But as Benjamin Herold points out in *Education Week,* "Google [is] under fire for data-mining student email messages."[293]

Again, the contradictory nature of the metaphysical God's omnipotence extends to the technological God's omnipotence. The collection of information stands at the center of Google's power. More specifically, Epstein reports that as of 2016, "More than 70 percent of Google's $80 billion in annual revenue comes from its AdWords advertising service"[294] This collection of data to target advertise for its clients of AdWords serves as the rationale for scanning Gmail users data.

With such complete power Google can offer educational institutions these services without charge. Although Google stated in August 2013, that "there is no ad-related scanning or processing in Google Apps for Education," Google was sued by students, who filed the suit on January 27, 2016, for collecting and using data about the students' use of non-educational services, including browser behavior, search history, YouTube viewing and search history, installed browser extensions and saved passwords.[295]

But do students have a choice in the matter? According to the dictates of free will, students technically have an option to consciously avoid using Gmail and the other apps, but like the limited spectrum of actual choice without consequences in theological terms, students must choose correctly. The correct choice means to use Gmail and any other required software or interface Google provides. Jackie Smith of the International Network of Activist Scholars and Alfredo Lopez notes that "74 of the top 100 universities use Google apps for their university communications and software applications"[296] Furthermore, they note that the "New York City School Department adopted Chromebook as part of its approved and supported tools in its 1800 schools"[297] In short, the limited nature of theological free will aligns with the limited nature of technological free will. Again, Hegel's contradictory God manifests in Google as the technological God because while the software benefits students and the institution, in general, it also virtually mandates the sharing of all information with Google.

In addition, Smith and Lopez mention that "according to leaked NSA documents, Google . . . cooperate[s] with the NSA PRISM surveillance program, which authorizes the U.S. government to secretly access data . . . without a warrant."[298] Attorney Stephanie A. DeVos examines this relationship in her study, "The Google-NSA Alliance: Developing Cybersecurity at Internet Speed." Also, the *Washington Post* reports that Google and the NSA had partnered in 2010.[299] In short, Google's omnipotence in creation of Gmail for the ultimate good extends into its inherent omniscience (and omnibenevolence, omnipresence, as well).

This investigation of Gmail is not to simply point out that everything Google propagates as good has an evil underbelly, but rather to emphasize that omnipotence involves the absorption of any evil attached to all creations for goodness. This holds true in the case of the theologians' assertions of God's omnipotence, and it holds true for the technological God, Google. In basic terms, if God does it, it is always good, regardless. If Google does it, it is always good, regardless. Basically, omnipotence means *all*-powerful. It even includes the power to make what is obviously evil (or at least problematic, unethical, immoral) part of the supreme good.

This rhetorical strategy proved effective in religious and now in technological enterprises. Jerry Mander notes in his book *The Case Against the Global Economy: And a Turn Towards Localization*:

> One could find similarly optimistic statements for every new technology that comes along. Those who emit such statements have nothing to gain from our learning the possible negative consequences of these new commodities, so we are left with a constant stream of best-case-scenarios and virtually no countervailing voice. As we have discovered, however, many manufacturers and industries, including nuclear, chemical, auto . . . are aware of serious negative outcomes of their technologies, but choose not to share these with the public and often hide them from investigative inquiry.[300]

Mander's analysis illustrates the central promotional method inherent in the behavior of sources of power. The only aspect that requires mention involves the moment when the object mass become aware of the negative aspects of a new technological creation. When they do, the goodness of the object absorbs the obvious negatives and what results constitutes mass allegiance and subservience (whether conscious or unconscious) to power because of the element of perpetual use and little alternative to do otherwise.

The Omnibenevolence of Google

God's power to make evil good presents an evident link to His omnibenevolence because it augments His other central attributes. Augustine states, "[God's] greatness is the same as His wisdom; for He is not great by bulk, but by power; and His goodness is the same as His wisdom and greatness, and His truth the same as all those things." [301] All of His attributes correspond to God's entire substance and His essence. Augustine's concept of God's goodness, which concerns His other attributes, characterizes an exacting and fundamental notion on the personality of God.

Similarly, Google's attributes overlap. Its creations, such as search, Gmail, and Apps for Education highlight the multifaceted nature of Google. The central aspect of God's omnibenevolence concerns His relationship to His creation. Because God is good, He cannot create anything that is not good. The essential character of goodness proceeds from creator to created. This causal link supports Anselm's theological ontology summarized as "God is that which nothing greater can be thought."[302] Logic breaks if God is not omnibenevolent. So, according to Augustine, God made everything good, whether plant life or human life, which pinpoints the central goodness of God. God only creates good, and so anything evil can be described as only being less good. Augustine uses the term greater good to provide a spectrum of goodness through God. He writes, "Every actual entity is therefore good; a greater good if it cannot be corrupted, a lesser good if it can be."[303] By positing God as perfectly good (omnibenevolent) above all else, Augustine comes to the challenge of evil and produces a cogent argument that defines evil as a "lesser good." Therefore, humans must be good regardless of producing evil in the physical world. Of all of creation, the human stands as God's image at the highest peak of His universal masterpiece, Earth.

Google creates the human. This operates as pure existential testimony of Google's omnibenevolence. The human embodies its finest creation. Search, Gmail, YouTube, Docs, Drive, Hangouts symbolize the creative force of goodness and bears fruit with its image-offspring by extension. Universal homogenized reproduction of assurance of unity through these creative vectors. McLuhan's insight reflects an essential notion of the technological God. He quotes Father John Culkin: "We shape our tools and thereafter our tools shape us."[304] The tools that Google creates shape us.

McLuhan generously includes the masses in the term "we," but it is not "we" who initially shape the tools. Google shapes the tools. "To shape" means to shape "by a process of careful thought." Google shapes its tools with constant revision. For example, B.J. Mendalson, author of *Social Media is Bullshit,* claims that if one hundred people view a YouTube video within the first ten minutes after its upload, an algorithm will "trigger" determining the success of the video.[305] The connection to the shaping of tools and tools shaping us appears obvious with Mendalson's example. A video upload enters a space of calculation that, in turn, maneuvers the upload through a tunnel of computation. Levy explains this tunnel of shaping. He writes, Google "gathers massive amounts of data and processes that information with learning algorithms to create a machinelike intelligence that augments the collective brain of humanity."[306] Levy's description is apt. Google collects information and develops sets of rules that determines its navigation. Levy eludes the accuracy of his proposal when he separates the "collective brain of humanity" from the learning algorithms. The learning algorithms cannot "augment" the collective brain of humanity because *they are* the collective brain of humanity. YouTube is the tool that is shaped by algorithms, which then shape the human. McLuhan's paradoxical reading of the technological tool offers the proper perspective to confirm the goodness of its creation through the creation of the human. Just as God's central creation is the human, the human is Google's central creation.

So, the human being becomes a single mass object from the creative tools Google shapes. Therefore, the positions of subject and object complicate because Baudrillard positions the mass(es) into a "double bind."[307] Baudrillard explains that the masses are "simultaneously summoned to behave like autonomous subjects, responsible, free, and conscious; and as submissive objects, inert, obedient, and conforming."[308] Google's nature benevolently requires (mandates) free will for its creation with a correlative element of its nature that requires submission. Essentially, this lives within the construction of Google. Technicians mechanically create the psycho-social environment which breeds this fundamental paradox. Incidentally, this paradox proves necessary to the concept of "omni" benevolence. At the level of the individual subject, the masses are simultaneously ordered to manifest their subjectivity through apprehending specific desires from a pre-selected range of "free" choices while the demand to be a complacent object matches the obligation for individual subjectivity. This epitomizes God's love that extends to the technological version of God.

Mike Gane illustrates Baudrillard's discussion on this relationship of power to the masses, which corresponds to the paradoxical demands of God's omnibenevolence. The graphic below shows that "Power" (Google) treats mass as both object and subject. Therefore, humans are commanded to exercise their subjectivity through free choices in entertainment, consumer items, fashion, and so on.

The command, itself, negates human subjectivity. Further, humans must choose from predetermined choices, which, in essence, makes humans a mass object. When humans resist and attempt to be individual subjects, Google treats them as objects. When humans behave as passive objects in resistance to subjectivity, Google treats them as subjective beings by offering more choice. This perpetual middle ground results in the object mass running on inertia.

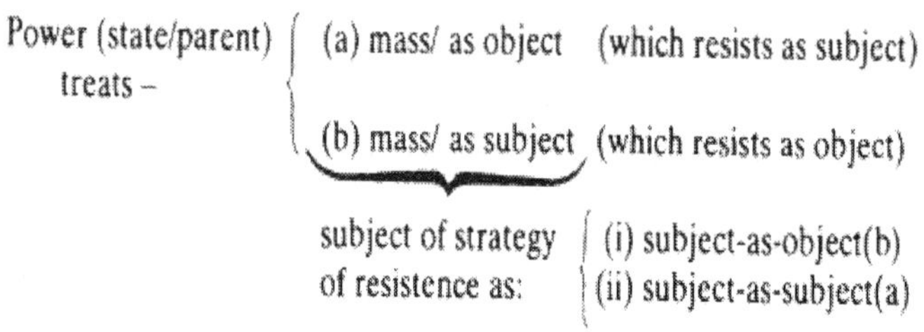

Image from Gane's *Baudrillard (RLE Social Theory)*

Again, Mendalson claims that if one hundred people view a YouTube video within the first ten minutes after its upload, an algorithm will "trigger" determining the success of the video. Therefore, the mass is directed to enjoy the freedom and entertainment of the innumerable videos for viewing. Once the mass unknowingly triggers an algorithm for a particular video, the video proliferates to the entire mass object. Then the video shapes the mass object. Using YouTube shapes the mass in terms of McLuhan's medium theory, but the content of videos also shapes the object mass in the contrived elements of popular human existence. For example, this occurs in fashion, dance, language (slang), political movements, conspiracy theories, etc. Therefore, the human is shaped by an algorithm that displaces the potential human subjectivity while it postures the splendor of free choice. The free choice itself is informed by love.

To continue with this point, although presented as an act of love, free will seems to function as an encoded endowment of God's omnibenevolence. For instance, humans associate within a community or a society. In the case of YouTube, the community is global and online. This makes free will a social activity. Like all social activities, certain regulations from the Symbolic register inhabit the space of formal social practice. Žižek, in his book *How to Read Lacan*, identifies the "empty gesture" or the "offer made to be rejected."[309] The capacity of free will to sustain the ritualistic practice of social engagement requires the use of these empty gestures. This maintains conceptually the fallacious underpinnings of Christian free will as well as the function of Google, in terms of freedom to choose in the global online society. Basically, homogeneity hides behind the vail of free choice.

Baudrillard evidences this premise in his examination of the "smallest marginal difference."[310] Essentially, the human subject receives the directive to express individuality through the slight differences in the commodities for purchase, such as the color of a shirt. But this choice simply reinforces the monopoly of a singular mode of being within the social realm (among other realms). He notes, "monopoly and difference are logically incompatible. If they can be combined, it is precisely because the differences are not differences and, instead of marking a person out as something singular, they mark rather his conformity with a code, his integration into a sliding scale of values."[311] Through consumption, this represents the codes in absorbing (purchasing) commodities. By analogy, through religion, this represents Christian free will. In other words, what appears as a free choice is merely a choice within narrow and fixed parameters.

Chomsky illustrates this by stating, "The smart way to keep people passive and obedient is to strictly limit the spectrum of acceptable opinion, but allow very lively debate within that spectrum."[312] Therefore, the consumer choices of Baudrillard and the "acceptable opinion" of Chomsky clearly support the idea of God's free will. Theologian Steven Harris confirms, "The Christian (especially Pauline / Augustinian) understanding of the nature of free will: when one chooses the good (and only the good), then one is truly free! But when one chooses evil, out of a free choice between good and evil, then one becomes bound to the evil and loses 'freedom of choice itself.'"[313] Henceforth, God decides what is good and what is evil, or the framework that surrounds the free choice is predetermined by God. Google proposes the same free will through its omnibenevolence.

To return to Lacan and Žižek, the choice within the structure of free will denotes an "empty gesture" or an act devoid of choice. To apply this to

Google, its search engine serves as a framework of which algorithms predetermine the choice of the mass (as object) who searches. Although Google returns thousands of choices for the masses to choose, the object works within the broader framework of Google's omnipotence. Former CEO of Google, Eric Schmidt told the Wall Street Journal, "I actually think most people don't want Google to answer their questions . . . they want Google to tell them what they should be doing next."[314] In the paradox of free will, Google develops algorithms to maneuver the masses to the next choice provided by and guided by Google. Furthermore, Žižek writes "In the subject's relationship to the community . . . you have freedom to choose, but on condition that you choose the right thing. If you make the wrong choice, you lose freedom of choice itself . . . this paradox arises at the level of the subject's relationship to the community to which he belongs."[315] The significance rests in the concept of the community. The masses must engage socially within the structure of Google, since Google has created the global online infrastructure.

In practical terms, Gmail serves as an example to illustrate the function of free will at the level of the worker or student (subjects of free choice and mass object). When an institution receives the creative force of Google with its ecosystem of enmeshed user interfaces, the mass must conform to the range of choices offered within that ecosystem. The free choice to abstain from the use of Gmail within an institution that requires all communication through the interface is the wrong choice. The consequence of rejecting communication through Gmail is expulsion from the institutional system.

Jeff Pruchnic elaborates on the empty gesture and its potential consequences attached to acceptance (or denial) of the offer. He writes, "That is, to resist means not to avoid the (illusion) of choice in the empty gesture, but to take it at face value; not to deny choice (or argue that it is being denied) but to revel in choice, to exploit the opportunity (falsely) offered as a genuine moment of agency and autonomy."[316] Zizek explains:

> In other words, the act of taking the empty gesture (the offer to be rejected) literally, to treat the forced choice as a true choice, is, perhaps, one of the ways to put into practice what Lacan calls 'traversing the fantasy': in accomplishing this act, the subject suspends the phantasmic frame of unwritten rules which tell him how to choose freely; no wonder the consequences of this act are so catastrophic.[317]

Lacan's traversing the fantasy correlates with Baudrillard's inertial masses who fulfill its forced choice by complying with the dictates of the empty gesture through aligning its movement and activity with the countless offers (requests) from Google. Žižek further clarifies "traversing the fantasy" when he writes:

> Fantasy renders and sustains the structure of the forced choice, it tells us how we are to choose if we are to maintain the freedom of choice, that is it bridges the gap between the formal symbolic frame of choices and social reality by preventing the choice, which, although formally allowed, would, if in fact made, ruin the system.[318]

Thus, potential consequences ensue, not only from breaking the unwritten rules of the forced choice, but also for following the rules to the letter. For example, the death of God is the consequence for following the Scholastic methodology of (scientific) rationalism to the letter. The object mass complied with the logical outcomes of rationality as a "free choice" and eventually saw the death of God through the requirement of accepting the empty gesture of the Scholastics and their clergy.

The symbolic meaning of the empty gesture holds together the structure. One's drive within the Symbolic register necessitates the obligatory movement toward the correct decision or right choice without the knowledge that the choice is right in order to fulfill the symbolic function of the arrangement. The predetermined correct choice further highlights the omnibenevolence of Google. Within the ecosystem countless auto-suggestions maneuver the mass object into a circuitry, informed by unconscious personal desire, to the place most appropriate. The symbolic element of the correct choice connects the circuit with the most appropriate click. Regardless, an inappropriate click provides a path toward the application of the forced choice because the pathway alters the mass to the predetermined point of (a) recovering. Google Maps illustrates this with directions. When one makes a turn that proves contrary to the instructions, Google will attempt to reroute the object toward the destination. Google search operates in the same manner. So does God. Therefore, the love for the object mass creates scenarios of predetermined movement along "correct" or "right" circuits in order to reify the all-inclusive pathway toward the total fulfillment of psychological (psychoanalytic) desire.

Suva Vaidhyanathan, author of *The Googlization of Everything*, relates this concept in practical terms when he writes, "If Google is the dominant way we navigate the Internet, and thus the primary lens through which we experience both the local and the global, then it has remarkable power to set agendas and alter perceptions. Its biases are built into its algorithms."[319] His basic assumption of operational power undergirds Google's Godly attributes in terms of omnipotence. The power to create a global infrastructure out of love for the object mass signals a total mediation of the human from which the human cannot "act" without Google. This melts into Google's omniscience as Eric Schmidt claims (confesses?) "We know roughly who you are, roughly what you care about, roughly who your friends are."[320] Similar to the structural guidelines of the Panopticon, the algorithm structurally enlists a system of total omniscience and, therefore, total omnipresence and, furthermore, total omnipotence. All of which prove unrecognizable since the structural arrangement predetermines these attributes. What Schmidt describes as a rough sketch of individuals within the mass object evolves into an absolutely accurate portrait of each human because Google's rough sketch trumps the reality of the actual human subject.

This proves to be the case because the human individual can no longer trace personal becoming without the various Google interfaces that are designed to create the individual human in its image. Baudrillard notes, "the opposing poles of determination vanish"[321] and with it the "minimal distance between cause and effect."[322] With Google's place as God, the human enters the Google ecosystem only to later understand (consciously or otherwise) that "I am as Google made me." All humans within the ecosystem adapt to its environment to the point where "there is no longer any imperative of submission to the model . . . [because] YOU are the model."[323] In biblical terms, "YOU are the image of God." The separation of cause and effect dissolves (the case with all binaries) to a constant cause and effect without any trace of which is which.

What is left is a total cause and a total effect, completely comprehensive. Vaidhyanathan summarizes, "[Google interfaces are] so closely tailored to reflect the choices we had already made that it could reliably predict how to satiate our established desires."[324] Hillis et. al. reinforce this when they write, "it is not the Cosmos [God] doing the predetermination but an information machine developed by individuals who believe that the 'truth' of hard data always trumps the 'illogic' of embodied realities that nonetheless do not easily yield to pattern recognition by artificial intelligence."[325] The truth of hard data recalls the motif of utopian scientific progress that founds the central precepts of Google's methodology. In the long term, the embodied realities will yield to pattern recognition by artificial intelligence because of the inherent breakdown, structurally devised, between the poles that separate the embodied human subject and the conceptual vagaries of artificial intelligence. The question is not, will artificial intelligence (machines) become more human, but rather will the human become more artificial (robotic / machinelike)? Again, before God made man in His image, man-made God in his (ideal) image (through the Word, the Symbolic).

The Omniscience of Google Underlies its Omnibenevolence

Google's omniscience functions paradoxically. Google is all-knowing as it concerns all information previously outside of Google, such as printed books. It also produces (stores or holds) all information and, henceforth, information is nowhere to be found outside of Google. As the creator of information it will always know all information. This extends to knowledge of all human individuals individually and all knowledge of the masses as object. But Google's knowledge is also produced by the object mass in a simultaneous moment in what Hillis et. al. identify as "the human-machine assemblage on which search relies."[326] While search gives information it also takes information that informs what future information it gives to the searcher.

One essential element of Google's omniscience includes the quest for universal knowledge. This knowledge base differs from the information collected from human search. Instead this knowledge base comes from books. Google attempts to "digitize all the books that have ever been printed since the time of Gutenberg,"[327] and through Google Books, humans can "search every book ever published."[328] Levy notes, "Of the estimated 33 million books that had been published, Google wanted all of them."[329] In order to set up this ambitious project / interface, Google tried to access all of the books in the Library of Congress, but the head of its Copyright Office, Marybeth Peters "saw red flags."[330] Therefore, Google set up an agreement with University of Michigan with the goal to digitize all 7 million volumes of its library. Several problems arose with Google's digitizing attempt, such as copyright, privacy, anti-trust, and censorship, which resulted in the 2005 lawsuits from the American Association of Publishers and the Authors Guild.[331] Regardless Google has digitized and continues to digitize millions of books.

The first important point that concerns Google's scanning of books involves its approach to the law as it pertains to a higher cause or a transcendent morality. Hillis et. al. explain that the "Google Book Settlement affair suggest[s] that . . . with respect to copyright at least . . . [Google] considers itself an authority morally compelled if not authorized to invent and impose new forms of legal understandings and ownership."[332] In essence, since Google's central objective revolves around the goodness embedded in its utopianesque goals for global technological perfection (unity), it can transform current "human" or "temporal" laws to elevate the entire creation. All humans benefit from Google's new moral guidelines in terms of copyright. Ironically, in 1995, "Sergey Brin . . . collaborated with fellow Ph.D. students and professors on a project involving automated detection of copyright violations."[333] Under copyright law, Google did not have the authority or permission to scan and make available, through Google Books, any printed text, but did so anyway. The attempt to create a complete library that is available for all Google users proves the nature of Google's elevated morality. When the goal is loftier than simple human copyright law, Google's decisions are justified in every case.

The justification to break human copyright law involves the higher goal of offering virtually unlimited scholarly (or otherwise) data / books through a convenient and user friendly search. Page mentioned, "It is really hard for scholars to work outside of their area of expertise because of the physical limitations of libraries."[334] Therefore, from Google's perspective, the ultimate and infinite good of producing a global digital library will open a new world to human scholars from the limitations of the physical. Furthermore, John Battelle, author of *The Search: How Google and Its Rivals Rewrote the Rules of Business and Transformed our Culture,* contemplates, "It is odd to think that seven years after they started a company to 'organize the world's information and make it universally accessible and useful,' Brin and Page find themselves pondering a role as the morality police for the global economy."[335] But their goal implies a distinctly Godlike morality of (apparent) contradiction and exceptionalism. To refer back to the ethical monotheistic God, Luther posits reason as a "gift from God"[336] and writes, "All laws have been produced by the wisdom and reason of men."[337] But God's Law, rife with conflict in human terms, forms the supreme justness that trumps human law. So, in terms of an approach to morality, Google sits above mere human law.

The ethical monotheistic God represents the closest representation of ultimately contradictory morality for the greater elevation of a greater purpose. For instance, in terms of offering censored versions of Google products, particularly Search, Google rationalized its entrance into the Chinese markets. Schmidt reasoned, "We concluded that although we weren't wild about the restrictions, it was even worse to not try to serve those users at all. We actually did an 'evil scale'"[338] The subtext of Schmidt's statement illuminates the standard rationale for problematic "Godly" inconsistencies because Google constructed and performed its own "evil scale" for itself and by itself to determine whether to do business in China and, more significantly, how to articulate the shaky justification for doing business in China.[339] Moreover, Schmidt presents Google as a service for users, thereby implying the sanctity of its purpose. Incidentally, Google shut down its search engine in China in 2010 and its other services in 2014. But it is preparing to return to China shortly.[340]

In fact, *New York Times* writer Nicholas Kristof composed an ironical and unintentionally satirical article entitled, "Will Google bring Freedom to China?" where he proudly declares, "In a conflict between the Communist Party and Google, the Party will win in the short run. But in the long run, I'd put my money on Google."[341] Kristof foreshadows the complete global omnipotence of Google coupled with Google's omnibenevolent motives, which are manifested in free will (as in freedom for China); but when China freely engages with Google, it will enter Google's totalizing ecosystem. Kristof also writes, "Eventually, a combination of technology, education, and information will end the present stasis in China."[342] Here Kristof reaffirms the utopian vision of Enlightenment progress for the betterment of the world, while Page tells Battelle, "I realized I wanted to invent things, but I also wanted to change the world. I wanted to get them out there, get them into people's hands so they can use them, because that's what really matters."[343] Battelle goes on to explain that Google "fundamentally changed the relationship between humanity and knowledge."[344] Essentially, the "education" and "information" (or knowledge) that will "end the stasis of China" comes from the power of Google to dictate the transmission of knowledge in both medium and content under the banner of progress and, more importantly, under the banner of love.

The paradox of Google's benevolence to create Chinese freedom underlies the central concept that God contains what appears as oppositional morality, which becomes easily reconcilable by the inherent essence or definition of God. To confirm, at one point Google held over 36% of the market share of search in China after just three years in the country.[345] Therefore, if / when Google returns to China, it is completely plausible that it will be as integrated into the daily Chinese experience as it is in the United States.

Google's omnibenevolence also involves its goodness to all people, regardless. In describing the metaphysical God, Anselm proclaims, "O good God, good to the good and to the wicked . . . your goodness is incomprehensible."[346] Therefore, God's omnibenevolence rests upon His goodness to all people, and His incapability to do anything evil. "Google Foundation," through Google Dot-org, serves as the prime example that Google, like the metaphysical God, is omnibenevolent.[347] For instance, Google mentions at *Google.org* that it donates over a billion dollars in grants and products to countless charitable non-profit organizations such as GiveDirectly, World Wildlife Fund, Consortium for the Barcode of Life, charity: water, DoSomething.org, and Malaria No More. The center point of Google's charitable giving revolves around the use of advanced technology to help improve earthly conditions for people. For instance, Google declares that it is "designing a world that works for everyone!"[348] Obviously, Google's uses its ability to intelligently design the globe so that all people, good or wicked, can participate in meaningful global activity.

Google calls these Impact Challenges. One such challenge to overcome is human disability. Google states, "The Google Impact Challenge: Disabilities aims to make the world more accessible for the 1 billion people living with disabilities."[349] Two such Google organizations are Mission Arm and Miraclefeet. As the names suggest, these non-profits enable humans with damaged or missing limbs to lead more productive lives. Both groups investigate how technology can be used to design, inform, and treat these humans. Mission Arm works with exiii, a prosthetic manufacturer, to use "3D printing" to construct a robotic limb.[350]

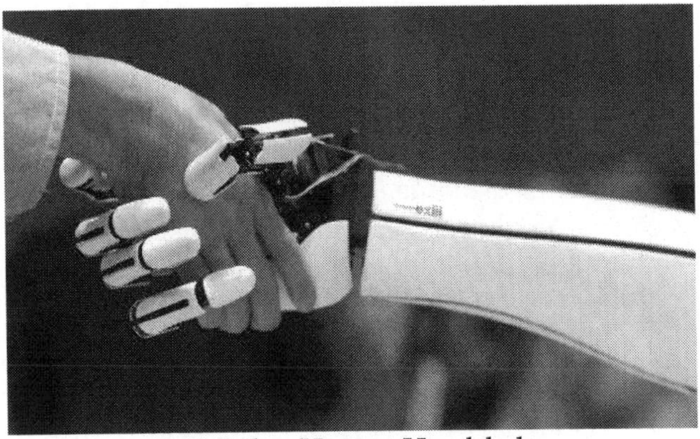

Exiii Robot Human Handshake.

Miraclefeet uses its support from Google to "improve clubfoot treatment worldwide by offering family support via SMS (Short Message Service), monitoring patient progress through updated software, and providing extensive online training to local clinicians."[351] The technological God, Google, offers those with disabilities the miraculous use of their limbs. Finally, Google provides support measures for those in India who suffer from leprosy. Apparently, India confirms "100,000 new cases every year."[352] Hence, Google's actions provide the necessary assistance to "ensure that a large number of people who suffer from leprosy maintain the ability to walk" ("Leprosy Mission"). These three examples are merely a glimpse into the goodness of Google toward humans.[353]

In terms of feeding the human, Google began the Hunger Relief Campaign that has provided more than "eight hundred thousand meals."[354] Global

Giving's Chief Business Officer Donna Callejon describes it as Google's way to "take a bite out of hunger."[355] She narrates, "Koro is a six-year old [malnourished] girl [from Mali] who arrived at A Child for All's orphanage without a home or family."[356] Koro saw the food[357] at lunch time and took the whole dish and ran away because "she didn't know that there would be another meal later."[358] Callejon adds, "It's hard to think that engineers and marketing managers 7,000 miles away in Mountain View, California are key to improving the life chances of Koro and other children."[359] Google's goodness to Mali also includes "building a school and a library."[360] According to Google, it gives help to refugees, as well. With its support for the International Rescue Committee, it "built an online information hub for refugees."[361] On the Google Dot - org website, one can see a picture of the "home refugee crisis" that resembles what Barthes's describes in *Mythologies* when he discusses the film *The Lost Continent*. He writes, "It is the same for the refugees, a long procession . . . making their way down a mountain . . . they are eternal essences of refugees."[362] Another nonprofit that Google backs is NetHope, and it is "Changing the world through the power of technology."[363]

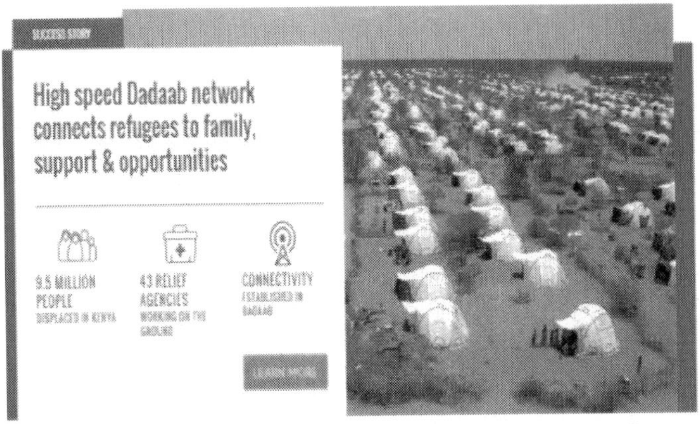

Refugees in Dadaab, Kenya, Africa.

With Google's goodness as the central support, NetHope set up an internet connection in a refugee camp in Dadaab, Kenya. NetHope reasons, "With a reliable Internet connection, people living and working inside the Dadaab camp are now able to learn basic ICT skills, utilize email and social media accounts to connect with friends and loved ones, [and] access online education."[364] In summation, Google freely gives the disposed and disenfranchised the opportunity to walk, eat, and use social media.

To further evidence Google's omnibenevolence, reporter *The Guardian's* Anna Bawden reports that "In the UK, 20 charities won grants ranging from £200,000 to £500,000 in 2013 and 2014. These included a project by the Royal National Institute for the Blind to develop smart glasses, as well as initiatives tackling youth homelessness . . . through technology."[365] Google gives sight to the blind and shelter to the homeless. To give sight to the blind recalls a moment when God the Son heals the blind man in Bethsaida.[366] After God the Son gives the blind man sight, he says to his disciples, "Whosoever will come after me, let him deny himself . . . and follow me."[367] The "smart glasses" Google lovingly provides allows the blind to see through (and like) Google sees. All are welcome in the Kingdom of God, even the blind, as long as they deny themselves. The exchange grows global and no longer requires a coming after on the part of the human subject. The coming after occurs at birth into the superstructure of Google's omnipresence. The exceptions exist as refugees, the disabled, the impoverished, and the "underdeveloped" Others, but they will no longer be exceptions.

Further, *WIRED* writer Issie Lapowsky reports that "Google is bringing free gigabit fiber[368] to public housing across the Unites States."[369] Again, to feed the poor means to feed the poor with online access and the technological infrastructure to facilitate entrance into the Google ecosystem.

The goodness of Google does not discriminate entrance into its kingdom. Lapowsky verifies, "Not only will it establish [Google's] Fiber [Network] as the Internet provider of choice for more Americans, but it will get more Americans actually using the Internet, which in today's world necessarily means becoming a Google user."[370] Even the wicked can experience Google's goodness. *USA Today* reporter Alexandra Mosher relates, "Maya, whose father is on a 25-year sentence in a California prison, was one of the many children who was able to send her incarcerated parent a video, thanks to an effort led by Google called #LoveLetters."[371] To reiterate, Anselm proclaims, "O good God, good to the good and to the wicked . . . your goodness is incomprehensible."[372]

Like the metaphysical God, the technological God, contains contradictions in its nature in terms of omnibenevolence. While it is evident that giving food to people who need food or enabling people who are lame to use their limbs represents a certain element of goodness, Google ultimately and permanently alters (creates) the entire sphere of human existence. When Google helps to provide food for a group, it also seizes the opportunity to transform (create) the people it helps to feed. In the case of Mali, the orphanage accepts the food donations, but must also accept the eventual / inevitable entrance into the Google ecosystem, through the Google school and library. Funds provided to robotics companies for prosthetics contribute to the overall advancement of the global technological empire and, specifically, in artificial intelligence. Offline refugees now become online algorithmic participants.

To repeat, Google says, "[We are] designing a world that works for everyone."[373] This sentence reveals the point of creation: "[We are] designing a world." *WIRED* writer Davey Alba words it in this way: "Google.org thinks it can engineer a solution to the world's woes."[374] Google's omnipotence in creation allows it to manifest its omniscience through technological devotion; it is motivated by its omnibenevolence and governed by its omnipresence.

Which resolves any conflict in Google's nature, and justifies a higher law for a higher cause.

To return to Google's omniscience, Google accesses and uses information collected constantly with its products. In a very practical sense, Google knows everything there is to be known. To review, God's creation provides the evidence for his omniscience. This entails a universal knowledge encompassing everything or as Brown describes it: "The eternal God knows all events as a timeless observer of them."[375] Also, Thomas offers the analogy: "For the knowledge of God is to all creatures what the knowledge of the artificer is to things made by his art."[376]

Finally, God's omniscience likewise manifests in the realm of fear and punishment. Therefore, God's omniscience entails knowledge of all events, especially those that pertain to His creation, and this knowledge lends to the potential for punishment. Google's omniscience follows the same dictates. Google's Apps for Education represents the efforts of Google to infiltrate each part of the object mass's mental and physical navigation through life.[377] Apps for Education includes the basic "free" services hundreds of millions use every single day. Gmail, Drive, Calendar, Docs, Sheets, Slides, and Vault inform the comprehensive usurpation of human subjectivity. These products, taken as objects in consumption, "determine a person's identity"[378] and denote "the objectification of the subject and the subjectification of the object."[379] This paradox epitomizes the situation Baudrillard refers to when he writes, "The mass realizes that paradox of being both an object of simulation and a subject of simulation."[380]

Baudrillard defines the human subject as "the person with its passions, its wills, its character."[381] Therefore, Google places human subjects into a subjective position of freedom to utilize these products, but simultaneously produces an object mass who homogenize through its place and mandatory participation in the circuit of standardized interfaces. Regardless of the "smallest marginal differences" of "personalization"[382] each human subject yields because Google's media screens overwhelm any subjective expression from its human users. For instance, Google Drive, when operated in the context of education, allows for unlimited data storage. This means that users upload diverse content into their own Drive accounts.

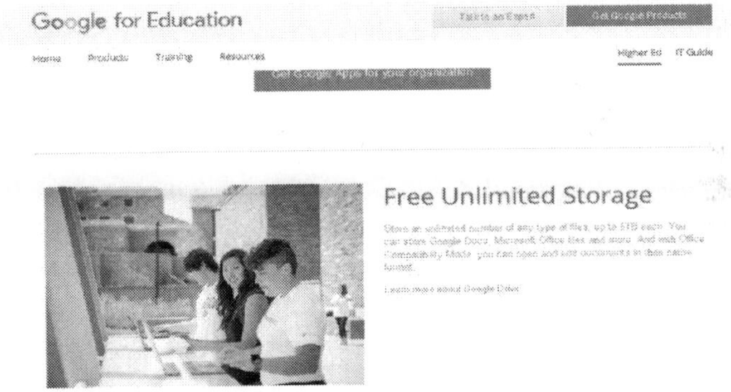

Screen Shot of Google Drive Unlimited from Google's Education Website.

The diversity of the content hints at a subjective experience; but the use of the service itself allows for the formation of the object mass. In reference to omniscience, Drive makes all its users' data easily accessible to Google. Google continues to expand its Classroom product, which began as a pilot program in May 2014.[383] Classroom is "free" to anyone with an Apps for Education account. Lapowsky explains that "Classroom allows teachers to set up a virtual classroom, invite students in, distribute worksheets, assign work, grade and return work, and collaborate with students on a document in real time. Classroom keeps track of what work has been turned in and automatically sorts it into Google Drive."[384] School Districts and individual schools who sign on to Google Classroom are referred to as Google Schools. These schools purchase at least one Chromebook for every two students.[385] Therefore, students use Google laptops with Google Apps in the context of learning about the world. This education involves Google as the prime mediator who oversees every exchange and interaction of its teacher and student users. History teacher Kaitlin Morgan explained, "We used Docs for notes, Draw for projects like collages. They created their own websites through Sites for a budget project, and I built quizzes and tests on Google Forms."[386] She represents the consensus viewpoint of teachers on the vast expansion of Google into educational institutions. Of course, the underbelly of the use of these Apps in schools consists of the fact that Google collects all of the data in all of the Apps.

To emphasize this fact, Google's (G Suite) terms of service read: "By using Google services, you acknowledge and agree that Google may access, preserve, and disclose your account information and any Content associated with that account."[387] There are a few caveats in accordance with Google's privacy policy like "governmental request," "potential violations," "technical issues," or "fraud," but with such broad stipulations, Google holds the power to know everything. Also, Google can change the terms of service at any moment. Obviously, this includes the ability to cause fear and to punish the users of these products. Furthermore, by eliciting the use of these products in the education of the young, Google assures its permanent place throughout the lifetime of the individual. The logical extension of this technology metaphorically places the student into the same space as the "Christian" from the time of the metaphysical God's dominance. The student trains to be a Google human from infancy. Hence, just as the Church produced the Christian, the Google School produces the Google person.

Google knows the Google person because Google creates the technology which creates the person. This offers full unencumbered knowledge of the students whose decision to use Google Classroom does not originate with them. In other words, it is not a subjective decision for the students. Administrators or teachers (technicians) partially make these decisions. But essentially, these decisions are made by those who carry a Google mind. The adults also utilize the interfaces daily outside of the educational context. Therefore, when Google initiates or advertises the use of these products (objects) in the school, the technicians already enter the decision with the Google brain. As the creator of the interfaces, Google understands the how and the why of the individual and capitalizes on this knowledge. This results in a total apprehension of the subjective experience. To reinforce the power of this omniscience, Google holds the individual in its grasp though blackmail in collusion with the governmental authorities who can enforce the law. But the governmental authorities also fall under the power of the omniscience of Google (and its blackmail), which grants Google power well above that of any bureaucrat or statist institution.

Like Foucault's carceral, the school presents a neo-technological space to detain the minds of the young within the Google ecosystem. Google sits at the very top of a hierarchy that positions all stakeholders in education into a rigid caste structure that envelopes the child, who sits in the lowest stratified position, as a virtual prisoner to the panopticonic interfaces. Concerning the major effect of the Panopticon, Foucault writes, "[It is] to induce in the inmate a state of conscious and permanent visibility that assures the automatic functioning of power."[388] The administrator sees the work of the teacher who sees the work of the students, and Google sees the work of all of these participants. All of the "subsidiary authorities"[389] can observe the student at all times. But again, Google can see *all activity all the time*. Most importantly, the young student learns and accepts the surveillance as well as lives through the experience under the integration of a complete ontological system of total knowledge. The logical development (outcome) of the Panopticon with the infusion of Google technology (creation) ushers in what Baudrillard might call "The End of the Panopticon."[390] This architectural means of surveillance evolves electronically / digitally into an entity that no longer separates the inmate from the prison guard (or the warden), but instead combines the roles of all parties into one central means of figurative information exchange.

In Baudrillard's words, "No more violence or surveillance: only 'information' and . . . simulacra of spaces."[391] Google Classroom provides a hyperreal classroom space of predetermined pseudoengagement where the central objective of education is to collect data on, not from, students. The teachers, the parents, and even the students, are eliminated from education through Google Classroom. In the case of omniscience, they are irrelevant to the process of the (pseudo)suprasensory structure. For emphasis, Khaliah Barnes, director of the Student Privacy Project of the Electronic Privacy Information Center (EPIC), warns, "When you're using free services, if you don't know what the product is, you are the product."[392] "Product" in the discourse of capital, "object" in the context of omniscience.

Google's omniscience extends to its Android Operating System. According to Google, "Android powers hundreds of millions of mobile devices in more than 190 countries around the world. It's the largest installed base of any mobile platform and growing fast, every day another million users power up their Android devices for the first time and start looking for apps, games, and other digital content."[393] One part of the Android OS includes Google Photos (also available on other operating systems). Like other products, Photos offer "Free Unlimited Storage" and "Easy Editing" for picture and videos ("Google Photos"). *Android Authority* writer Simon Hill asks, "Google Photos: Should you be worried about privacy?"[394] He goes on to explain, "when you upload your photos you are giving the tech giant license to 'host, store, reproduce, modify, create derivative works, communicate, publish, publicly perform, publicly display and distribute' those photos."[395] Google owns the photos and videos once they are uploaded. More relevant to the argument lies the fact that even if one does not upload a photo, Google still stores the data on its servers. Huffington Post Senior Tech Editor Damon Beres confirms, "Google Photos is so good at storing your pictures online, you might not even realize it's doing it."[396] He goes on to say that even if one uninstalls the app "Google Photos . . . enable[s] a general function on your device that stores your pictures online regardless of the app being on your phone."[397]

Henceforth, Google in its role as God contains all of the masses visual data. Basically, the human is in Google and Google is in the human. As Luke 17:21 states, "Neither shall they say, lo here! or, lo there! for, behold, the kingdom of God is within you."[398]

The Kingdom of God is Google's ecosystem. The mass object resides within it and it resides within the mass object.

To elaborate, McLuhan claims that, "Faced with information overload, we have no alternative but pattern-recognition."[399] Paradoxically, McLuhan posits "pattern recognition" as the only way out of the "maelstrom" of advanced technological culture. Ironically, Google explains it "uses pattern recognition to make sense of images."[400] It continues, "a computer might be trained to recognize the common patterns of shapes and colors that make up a digital image of a face. This process is known as facial detection."[401] This bridges the gap between the metaphysical God who numbers the hairs on your head (*King James Version*, Luke 12:7) to the technological God who "trains" its computers to know the facial structure of each human through "detailed face geometry maps."[402]

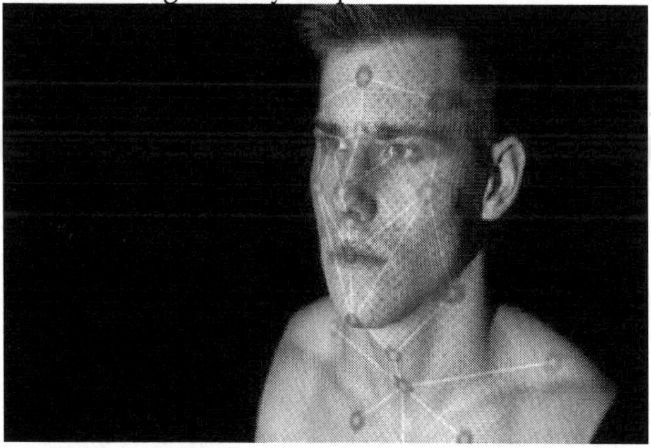

Face Scanning by John Lamb in *Fortune* magazine article.

Google is God

Google owns the images of the masses, which represents Google's image, and dictates the social mediation of the object mass. French Theorist Guy Debord lucidly explains this concept of mediation of images through the Godlike spectacle when he writes, "The spectacle is not a collection of images; rather, it is a social relationship between people that is mediated by images, . . . [and] the spectacle is the material reconstruction of the religious illusion."[403] A close reading of Debord offers the precursor to Baudrillard's more relevant *Simulacra and Simulation* in terms of how the image or the construction of the image precedes the image, itself. Therefore, essentially, Google follows the tradition of scientific rationalism and collects and analyzes visual data to categorize each image into prefabricated descriptors (genetic or otherwise) that are further categorized to the point where every image that makes up the object mass combines with every other image that makes up the object mass until all images homogenize / (de)metamorphosize into the image of Google, itself. In actual fact, the object mass is the image of Google all along because when the image enters Google's ecosystem it cannot exist outside of its omniscient ecosystem.

The human photo transposes the lucent barriers of the screen to forgo its own subjectivity "as a stockpiling of information and of messages, as fodder for data processing" and the "precession of reproduction over production."[404] To produce the photo stands irrelevant to its reproduction within the circuitry of Google's eco-science. All the separating markers of physical human pattern land symmetrically in the center of a power spectrum that leaves each individual human subject defined by a Google whose image (imaginary) structure concretely illuminates objectively. The captivation software, as an act of creative power, invokes a specialized minute distinction "which renders the generation of identical beings possible, though there is no possibility of a return to an original being."[405] Google photos brings the image to a place where it overcasts the private, sentimental, moral, and familial in the personal realm to the public, integral, dutiful, and universal field of the omniscient realm(s) God / Google.

For instance, David Arnott, editor of *The Business Journal,* in his article, "Google Photos may be Uploading your Pics, Even if you Don't Want It To" complains, "Google had access to pictures of my daughter and used that access to develop information, without my knowledge, about what she looks like and where she spends time . . . [and there] isn't much users can do to police this sort of activity."[406] Arnott resigns to the immutable fact that within the Google universe, human subjectivity lives as part of its own objectivity. The subjective event of putting oneself into the photo image through the Android OS device slides comfortably into the photo as official object. The gaze transforms into the technical identification of the Google pattern recognition to "develop information" that will later (almost simultaneously) prescribe a revision in the abundance of ever increasing knowledge. Therefore, at present (at future), Google is omniscient and simply becomes more omniscient because knowledge cannot exist outside of Google. The photo outside of Android (or the technological framework) has disappeared.

Google Photos

Photos. For life.

Screenshot from "Google Photos: Free up Space" Commercial.

Baudrillard substantiates: "The absolute loss of the image, bodies that cannot be represented, either to others or to themselves, bodies enucleated of their being and of their meaning by being transfigured into a genetic formula or through biochemical instability: point of no return, apotheosis of a technology that has itself become interstitial and molecular."[407] The life of the photo (image) continues in Google, but what is lost is the human distinctly separated from the biometrics that inform facial recognition. The Dionysian is absorbed into the advanced modes of scientific innovation where the actual disappears into the virtual. When Google expresses, "Photos. For Life." It articulates the reality of the infinite and immortal storage of the photos and more aptly the mechanism for survival. The human is not living until Google creates a geometric map of the human subject in order to confirm its biological existence. Inversely, the mapping of the face effectively kills the subject's freedom to transform in the Google ecosystem.

Google's omniscience extends to the use of pattern recognition for identifying speech through Voice Search. On its Privacy and Terms page it explains, "Voice Search allows you to provide a voice query to a Google search client application on a device instead of typing that query.
It uses pattern recognition to transcribe spoken words to written text."[408] Moreover, it continues, "We send utterances to Google servers in order to recognize what was said by you. We keep utterances to improve our services, including to train the system to better recognize the correct search query."[409] So Google hears what a human says and keeps whatever the human says on its servers. *PCWorld* contributor Chris Hoffman confirms, "Google captures and keeps all the voice searches, voice actions, and voice dictation activities you perform on your phone. It stores this with your 'Voice and Audio Activity,' which is tied to your Google account and used on Android, in Chrome, and in Google's apps on IOS."[410] As this technology advances, Google specifically recognizes with almost total accuracy the distinct voice of each human. Google knows all human voices.

Moreover, *WIRED* writer Robert McMillan describes how this works. He writes, "When you talk to Android's voice recognition software, the spectrogram of what you've said is chopped up and sent to eight different computers housed in Google's vast worldwide army of servers. It is then processed using neural network models."[411] In a circular arrangement of discovery, Google uses the structure of the human brain as a means for a synthetic "brain" to decipher a centrally individual human trait, the voice. As the human enters Google's voice recording arrangement, the brain of the human conforms to the technological medium; therefore, Google both uses and changes the human brain. Carr clarifies this idea with this explanation, "The recent discoveries about neuroplasticity . . . tell us that the tools man has used to . . . extend his nervous system . . . have shaped the physical structure . . . of the human mind. Their use has strengthened some neural circuits and weakened others."[412] Google identifies this software development as "neural network algorithms."[413] Neural network algorithms support a "computerized learning system that behaves like the human brain." Again, according to McLuhan, "We shape our tools and thereafter our tools shape us." Google, in its omniscience, creates algorithms based on the neural features of the human brain, which then transforms the neural features of the human brain to conform to Google's ecosystem media.

Google's explanation implies that the human must initiate the communication through Voice Search by saying, "Ok, Google." This places the human into a subjective position. But this fails to cover the actual usage of Voice Search. Andrew

Griffin, Journalist for the *Independent* makes clear that Google Voice Search "records and keeps conversation people have around their phones."[414] Google is omnipresent, which works with its omniscience, in voice recognition. Griffin reiterates, "Google could have a record of everything you have said around it for years . . . the company quietly records many of the conversations that people have around its products."[415]

Swedish IT entrepreneur Rick Falkvinge supports Griffin's assertion and notes that "Google will still start recording audio at random times and send it to Google's servers, when it picks up something it thinks sounds like 'Ok, Google' from a conversation."[416] In short, Google Voice Search enables Google to hear and store everything an individual says. While it is clear that Google has the capability to do this, it may refrain from doing so. Although Google holds the power for total omniscience, it does not necessarily mean that Google *manifests* this attribute all the time. Google can hear, recognize, record, and store every "utterance" from every individual at all times, but may not actually do so. This fact does nothing to diminish Google's omniscience.

To further facilitate Google's omniscience, it plans a future with driverless cars. Obviously, a human within a car controlled by Google software and navigated through Google Maps indicates a very specific form of omniscience. Basically, Google controls movement and knows where one travels. With Android software on all human devices, Google already knows the location of the human. Through Google Maps use on the Android device (and on non-Android devices), Google knows the route the human takes or plans to take. Generally, Google explains the best route to take. Again, as an overlap to Google's omnibenevolence, the goal for the fully self-driving car is "to transform mobility by making it easier, safer, and more enjoyable to get around,"[417] and further that "there are many people who are unable to drive at all who could greatly benefit."[418] As of now, the Google Self-Driving Car maneuvers its way through traffic with both human and manual controls; but Google plans to "remove these manual controls from the prototypes because our vehicles are ultimately designed to operate without a human driver."[419] One can add the major implication that the vehicles are ultimately designed to operate without a human (no passenger required).

The Google Self-Driving Car works in cohort with its counterpart, Google Maps. *Android Authority* writer Joe Hindy relays that "Google has been really on top of navigation . . . [and] Google Maps is better than pretty much everybody."[420] Like other services, Google offers its Maps for free. In return, the human, in Foucauldian terms, reinforces Google's omniscience by utilizing the Maps app. Google mentions that Maps includes comprehensive maps of 220 countries and territories as well as "detailed business information on over 100 million places."[421] It also lists the total number of installs on devices at one to five billion. *The Guardian* reporter James Ball notes the extent of Google's knowledge. He writes, "it effectively means that anyone using Google Maps on a smartphone is working in support of a GCHQ [Government Communications Headquarter or the British equivalent of the NSA] system."[422] Also according to Hindy, the human can install a variety of GPS apps for use with Android OS. Therefore, regardless of whether the app is produced by Google, such as Maps, or a non-Google navigation app, Google still knows the whereabouts (and activities) of all humans through its Android OS.

Appropriately, McLuhan famously declares, "Since Sputnik and the satellites, the planet is enclosed in a man-made environment that ends 'Nature' and turns the globe into a repertory theatre to be programed."[423] The Global Positioning System or the Global Navigation Satellite System took Google above the earth and into the heavens to program the world in its techno-centric image.

The human subject as a product of nature transforms into the human object on display for contribution to the algorithm. For instance, Maps provides a trip to other areas of the universe. It brags that with Google Maps the human can "check out the Milky Way, make a pit stop at Mars, and view the face of the moon. No spaceship required."[424] So, through the Google interface, the human sees these areas as pictured by Google. The former starry heavens now live as images though Google Maps. No telescope required, either.

Google Earth additionally adds a layer to Google's omniscience. In his book, *How Google Works,* former Google CEO Eric Schmidt describes the goodness that works alongside the knowledge in terms of Hurricane Katrina. He writes, "When Hurricane Katrina ravaged the US Gulf Coast . . . Google Earth had been on the market for only about eight weeks."[425] Then he adds, "But when the hurricane hit it . . . Google launched over eight thousand up-to-the-minute satellite images . . . [that] helped rescue workers . . . [and helped] agencies [to] distribute relief supplies and later aided survivors in deciding whether or not to return to their homes."[426] The altruistic benefits of Google Earth show Google's true omnibenevolent character. In fact, the Google Blog features countless images of global natural disasters, such as the Kumamoto earthquake and the Erskine fire in California.

Another example of Google's omniscience conjoined with its omnibenevolence comes from the "real" life story of Saroo Munchi Khan. Similar to the narratives from Google's charitable practice from Google dot org, the story of Saroo provides another global (third world) tale of Google's goodness. *Vanity Fair* contributor David Kushner narrates, "Separated from his older brother at a train station, five-year-old Saroo Munchi Khan found himself lost in the slums of Calcutta. Nearly 20 years later, living in Australia, he began a painstaking search for his birth home, using ingenuity, hazy memories, and Google Earth."[427] Apparently, Saroo began to evaluate his life after a period that included a "bad break up" and a lot of "partying." According to Kushner, "That's when he went to his laptop and launched Google Earth."[428]

Eventually, with Google Earth, Saroo reunites with his mother in India.

In addition, Google made efforts through its Earth app to help "an indigenous tribe, the Surui, map deforestation in their area of the Amazon,"[429] and uses its "neural networks to scour Google Earth in search of [more] deforestation. [Also Google] . . . can track agricultural crops across the globe in an effort to identify future food shortages."[430] In fact, *WIRED* writer Cade Metz confidently announces that "paired with AI and VR Google Earth will change the planet[!]"[431] Essentially, Google Earth moves from seeing the planet to knowing the planet to changing the planet. Of course, this echoes all of the visions supported by the advent of rationality from previous spirituality. It also fully evidences Google's power to create *what* the human sees of earth and *how* the human sees the earth. Finally, it illustrates the construction of the earth in Google's image by way of Google's omniscience and omnibenevolence.

Lastly, Google Earth enables humans to "explore the world from the palm of your hand"or "without leaving your desk."[432] As the general mediator of information, one can see the planet from Google's perspective through the screen. The mystery surrounding the surface of the earth and aesthetics of the heavens are no longer a mystery since the image displays real-time three dimensional vantage points from over thirteen thousand satellites. As Metz relates, "Google Earth is a nice way to look at the planet, not to the mention Mars, the Moon, and the heavens."[433] The reality of the place in time or the time in place no longer lags, but rather exists in the image of the real. Rescue workers in Louisiana play their role in the digital display mediated by the satellite and Google. From a distance, the human sees the global events through Google's interface and, thus, Google creates the global event for the human to consume. In essence, Google plays the Godly role of mediator to the reality of the catastrophe (that needs charity) and manifests its omniscience by, not only seeing all events all the time, but also labeling, defining, and explaining the events with(in) its ecosystem. Google Earth offers an all-inclusive package for human pseudoinvolvement in the world.

Other Google endeavors highlight its totalizing knowledge and power. In 2014, Google purchased its own satellite company, Skybox, a "startup that uses cube satellites to take more frequent and higher resolution photos from the skies."[434] Skybox now calls itself Terra Bella and looks to complete the puzzle of the world.[435] Its mission statement reads as follows: "We work alongside experts that have created geospatial data to serve billions of users and have the expertise to access data streams that complete the puzzle. It's a beautiful world and it's telling us a story. Are you listening?"[436] The object mass may not be listening, but it can be assured that Google listens.

The story the earth bears tells of technological and scientific advancement that recalls Zarathustra's perspective of the scientist who studies the brain of the leech. In other words, every tiny aspect of earthly existence comes under the microscope of the Google satellite. Google's Terra Bella boasts, "Our satellites offer a unique look at how our world is evolving, and how we can make positive changes in it."[437] For instance, Google tracks mining development in Mongolia and relates, "This data can be used . . . [to] systematically track development of projects in remote areas."[438] Under the banner of its goodness, no area, however remote, goes unnoticed by Google for the benefit of the object mass. Moreover, the scientists and engineers herald:

> While our satellites are zipping around the earth . . . [they are controlled] through a Chrome browser in our Mission Control Center capturing high-resolution imagery and downloading it to Google Data Centers for processing and storage. From there, the imagery is processed with a suite of processing algorithms allowing our team to then extract any useful information from the imagery to recognize patterns and help solve real problems.[439]

The term "real world" means the world according to Google and not necessarily the "real" world. A more accurate term is Baudrillard's "hyperreal" world.

Finally, Terra Bella offers the seventeenth century rationale and future utopian promise that still dominates Western culture when it states, "Through approaching daily global activity as the world's largest data science problem, we want to change the way we look at the world."[440] The obvious subtext conveys the fundamental change in how the world ought to be looked at by and through Google. Daily global activity, when identified as a "science problem" includes the analysis of every aspect of life. The human or object mass serves as the brain of the leech to Zarathustra's scientist. More importantly, Google is omniscient through its use of satellites.

To further continue its position as God, Google utilizes other objects that facilitate omniscience and omnipotence, through its omnibenevolence. One such object is "Google's Magic Internet Balloon."[441] Officially known as Project Loon,[442] Google intends to fill the sky with balloons that carry the technology to provide internet for millions who live in rural areas.

The Google Balloon from Surabhi Agarwal in *The Economic Times*.

Eventually, Google looks to launch balloons above rural India every thirty minutes to continuously support the "loon network."[443] The choice of rural India supports Google's goodness as *CNET* editor Daniel Van Boom notes, "Eight hundred and eighty million [Indians] live in rural conditions or poverty."[444] Plus, as one government official claims, "We are trying to test the effectiveness of Loon in the interiors of the country, since there is already ample connectivity in urban areas."[445] Naturally, the urban Indian population uses Google more than any other search engine as Google controls 96% of the search market in India (as of 2015).[446] Now the rural poor of India can join the urban population of India to access Google's ecosystem and gain entrance into the global network that informs Google's omniscience and consolidates its omnipotence. Another floating (or flying) technological object Google employs are the Google drones of Project Wing.[447] Project Wing announces, "We're building the next generation of automated aircraft, and working toward the day when these vehicles deliver everything from consumer goods to emergency medicine, a new commerce system that opens up universal access to the sky."[448] In September 2016, some "lucky Virginia Tech students . . . [got] their Chipotle fix"[449] as Google drones dropped the food from the sky into the crowd of hungry students. The drones not only feed humans, but help the climate because they take delivery vehicles off the road, which waste about "3.1 million gallons"[450] of fuel a year.

Furthermore, Astro Teller, CEO of Google X, the research and development factory now simply known as X, theorizes, "What excited us from the beginning is that if the right thing could find anybody just in the right moment they need it, the world might be a radically better place."[451] Teller implies that one can receive an immediate answer to one's request (prayer); ask and you shall receive (Matthew 7:7). Eventually, one might only think of an object, and Google will deliver it. Oliver Burkeman, writer for *The Guardian*, adds, "A search engine for the physical world is of limited use if it only serves up online photos of whatever you're looking for. A Google drone network could bring you the thing itself, almost as instantaneously as the search box delivers electronic results."[452] With the other objects and interfaces in Google's ecosystem, its drones represent the physical inclusion of universal connectedness whereby when the human enters text the drone shortly arrives. More accurately, the drone is always already there and precedes the human action of entering text.[453]

Daydream View allows the human to see the screen of the smart phone up close with a total virtual setting. The human lacks the capability to see peripherally. Everything on the screen explodes in color in the vision of the human. Sound funnels in and surrounds the human so that all sensory data comes from a single technological source that swarms around the human. The outside disappears, collapsed by the inside of the virtual world. This hyper-simulated reality overwhelms the primordial

Real since signifiers do not exist in their basic form. New signifiers erupt under the weight of promised new worlds. Google exclaims, "When your phone's screen becomes your big screen, you can get fully immersed in your favorite shows, movies, VR videos, and more."[454] It offers subjectivity with its command to "Take Control."[455] The injunction to grab individual subjectivity cannot be refused. The subjective human must oblige while shifting to the role of object mass as explained in Baudrillard's paradoxical "double bind." The only choices available to the human remain within the limitations inherent within the technological object. Žižek reiterates, "He must choose what is already given to him."[456] Google commands, "Daydream View's intuitive and expressive controller transforms with your imagination."[457] The imagination of the object mass becomes transformed by Google or in more accurate terms, created by Google.

Google's Omnipresence

All of the previously reviewed Google activities strongly support Google's omnipresence. As explained earlier, the metaphysical God is omnipresent. To be more specific, God's omnipresence is what the central theologians refer to as "derivative" omnipresence. This means that "God, considered apart from his standing in some relation or relations to objects that are themselves located at place fundamentally, could nevertheless be located at place."[458] Or basically that God is in all places at all times even in the same place as something or someone else. To summarize the Scholastic theologian Thomas, "It belongs to God to be present everywhere, since He is the universal agent, His power reaches to all being, and hence He exists in all things."[459] Google is also present everywhere and exists in all things. Again, *all* of the previously discussed Google products describe Google's omnipresence. Simply put, Google's presence abounds everywhere. The object mass cannot exist without the interaction of / with Google. Google is here with the human at every moment.

As it relates to omnipresence, the Google ecosystem serves as an environment which surrounds the object mass and to which the object mass contributes by participation. Although the ecosystem appears overtly through various signs of real interaction (typing text, for instance), its central all-encompassing circuitry actually remains invisible to the human. McLuhan offers a succinct explanation that concerns the invisibility of technological environments. He writes, "Environments are not passive wrappings, but are, rather, active processes which are invisible. The groundrules, pervasive structure, and over-all patterns of environments elude easy perception."[460] McLuhan's assertion of the invisible omnipresence of the technological environment especially applies to the most advanced and highly developed spaces. Therefore, the intensity of daily and constant engagement with technological objects (media) correlates with the level of technological (in)visibility. Mander reinforces

McLuhan when he notes, "Because technology is now everywhere apparent, pervasive, and obvious, we lose awareness of its presence."[461] Omnipresence reflects a reality where the existence of the omnipresent weaves itself into the fabric of daily life. In the case of Google, the Android OS on the billions of cellular phones simply exists in the background of everyday life. The object mass loses touch with the referential concept of the operating system that lives within the phone and, furthermore, mediates each interaction for each human on each day of each life. In the short term, the object mass may recognize the omnipresence of Google and may even comment on its omnipresence; but after that short period, Google simply exists everywhere without any conscious engagement (critical or otherwise) with Google from the object mass. Mander continues, "Once we accept life within a technically mediated reality, we become less aware of anything that preceded it."[462] In the case of the Kenyan refugees, they will initially perceive the entrance of Google into their collective space, but soon after, Google will transparently hover over their daily lives without any significant thought or reflection upon the omnipresence of the technology. In the more advanced world, Google has already accomplished this feat and is totally omnipresent.

To elaborate, Mander further writes, "We live our lives in reconstructed . . . environments; we are inside manufactured goods."[463] By analogy, the contemporary conception of the house, for instance, becomes omnipresent as a location of shelter. It is always there around the human. Houses simply exist as part of the landscape and no longer as additions to a previous landscape. The house simply is, and the object mass simply lives in houses. Similarly, Google's ecosystem simply exists as part of everyday existence or as an afterthought in daily life. The idea of life without Google loses any kind of reference conceptually. The object mass can no longer conceptualize life without Google because it does not conceive Google as a separate construction any longer. Google is within the object mass, but more notably, the object mass is within Google. Mander's "manufactured goods" that contain the object mass include all of Google's media products. Just as the object mass must live in houses or suffer the indignity of homelessness, it must also live in Google or suffer the indignity of Googlelessness . . . while simultaneously and *unconsciously* assuming that both houses and Google are fundamentally and immutably natural to human existence. This is the height of omnipresence.

At the heart of Google's omnipresence lies the creation of a space where reference to the previous space dies. Baudrillard expounds on this relational concept of omnipresence. Following McLuhan, he claims, "[Technological media] has evolved into a . . . closed system of models of significations."[464] He calls this "mass mediaization"[465] the large scale production, proliferation, and usage of technological mediums (media) that cover the landscape and close the system for entry by any opposition. Once the environment becomes totalized by these media, the media becomes invisible. Australian Scholar Peter Dallow clarifies, "Baudrillard warned that there is no worse mistake than taking the real for the real."[466] Thus, Google's media (search, Gmail, YouTube, Android OS, etc.) cover the referential real and become acknowledged as the real, but in truth, are merely the hyperreal. Dallow resumes, "Progressively the media . . . have replaced a lived sense of our world,"[467] and what were once "science fantasies" are now "technological fact, so that they now appear as the logical expression of contemporary consciousness, and of how we inhabit our lived world."[468] Consequently, the object mass in developed spaces lose their identification with anything previous to Google and now live within a naturalized omnipresent ecosystem. Conversely, those in underdeveloped spaces (rural India, Kenya, Mali, etc.) will lose their identification of a previous landscape without Google and enter Google's omnipresent space, and subsequently, lose all reference to the previous lived space. In Baudrillard's theory, this constitutes the covering of the real by the hyperreal, which then becomes the virtually real. At this stage, it becomes invisible.

This illustrates a crucial point of Google's omnipresence as the technological God because the world, as the creative activity of Google, becomes natural and, therefore, out of sight. This aligns with Foucault's claims about the prison. He asserts:

> One can understand the self-evident character that prison punishment very soon assumed.

> In the first years of the nineteenth century, people were still aware of its novelty; and yet it appeared so bound up and at such a deep level with the very functioning of society that it banished into oblivion all the other punishments that the eighteenth-century reformers had imagined.[469]

Google's omnipresence develops a self-evident character after only a short time within its ecosystem. Once it appears as a self-evident element of nature, the awareness of its novelty disappears. Reality, previous to Google, held the basic concepts and ideas of scientific and technological utopian advancement to the point that all new forms (Google) were readily accepted (whether purposefully or not) by the object mass.

Therefore, the entrance of Google into a system that held this transcendent and comprehensive attitude toward science and technology appears natural. Just as the eighteenth century punishments were banished into oblivion by the newly self-evident nineteenth century forms, so too the previous ways of being in the world are quickly banished by the Google ecosystem of being. As Foucault reports, in order for the prison to function with the utmost effectiveness, it must utilize "omnipresent surveillance, capable of making all visible, as long as it could itself remain invisible."[470] Google's omnipresence hides in plain sight and serves as a hyperreal naturalized formality of being within the confined space (Google's ecosystem) where the object mass resides without conscious awareness of being inside a carefully constructed environment. This reality quintessentially relates to the Kenyan refugees who consciously live in confinement, but who unconsciously reside in Google's environmentally omnipresent confinement.

To fully articulate this omnipresence in terms of Lacanian psychoanalysis, Žižek comments on the explanation of former Unites States Secretary of Defense Donald Rumsfeld on the question of "weapons of mass destruction" in Iraq. Basically, Rumsfeld mentions "known knowns," "known unknowns," and "unknown unknowns."[471] Žižek points out, "what [Rumsfeld] forgot to add was the crucial fourth term: the 'unknown knowns,' the things we don't know that we know, which is precisely, the Freudian unconscious, the 'knowledge which doesn't know itself,' as Lacan used to say."[472] The object mass within Google fails to conceive of its status, but knows its location nonetheless. Google's environment proves so invasive in presence that the knowledge of this presence dissolves in daily interaction and navigation within the environment.

But Google's omnipresence as an "unknown known" of the object mass highlights a more obscene element embedded in the concept of the metaphysical God as well as Google. In psychoanalytic terms, the human resides unconsciously aware of its spatial constraints, but cannot bear this harsh reality. Therefore, the mythologizing elements of Google's omnibenevolence serves to sublimate the unconscious knowledge of Google's omnipresence. Žižek further explains that the "unknown knowns" represent the "disavowed beliefs, suppositions, and obscene practices we pretend not to know about."[473] To pretend that Google exists as a benign force for technological progress occurs in the realm of Lacan's Symbolic register, which is "everything collected in our psyche from our experience. It is our parents and friendships, our social norms and taboos, our gods and demons."[474] In fact, the entire faith in the utopian promises of science through technological advancement already resides (has been implanted) within this part of human subjectivity through a symbolic chain of signifiers that ignites the pseudo-presence of the Real. In order to maintain the fantasy of the ([im]possible) Real, the object mass must continue to not know what it knows.

Moreover, the essence of omnipresence dictates that the knowledge of presence must be misapprehended or else the entire foundation of conviction loses all of its validity. In practical terms, the object mass must continue to utilize every facet of the Google ecosystem without critically engaging with Google, itself. To consciously concede to the omnipresence of Google means to "traverse the fantasy" toward institutionalization. As reviewed earlier, the fantasy of God resides within the small overlap of space primarily designated as an unconscious meeting place for the Symbolic, the Imaginary, and the Real. When the human decides that Google bears the signifier, omnipresent, the ascension of Google as the master-signifier paradigmatically enunciates the central assumptions implanted within the unconscious, which insists. The word then enters the field of observation through the subjective gaze of the individual.

For example, Google enters as the master-signifier to produce the Real within the framework of the natural world with its "Consortium for the Barcode of Life."[475] It designates the living beings as the object-as-other through the sublimation of knowledge and conservation. The identification of each individual animal from each species through the use of the digital "barcode" signifier allows Google to serve as the omnipresent mediator for the natural environment. Google dot org reports "A DNA barcoding library [allows] law enforcement officials to easily identify illegal trade species and better protect the world's most endangered wildlife."[476] Reports from Mexico, South Africa, Kenya, and Nigeria reinforce Google's essential entrance into the space of the "other" in order to traverse the "fantasy of the phantasm, which structures the relation to the other."[477] Therefore, the ethical attempt to subjectify the animals in the spaces outside of the institutional Symbolic works as an extension to subjectify the human in those same spaces. This conceptually counteracts the intention to bring into the field of the Real or bring out the Real from the unknown, the other. The use of barcode fulfills the Imaginary function that unsuccessfully allows for the convergence of the interrelational subjects. Through this core subjectifying act, Google, in turn, creates its subjective opposite and delimits the allowance of fantasy to manifest into sublimative fruition.

When the objectified other grasps the entire impetus for total information that comes from Google, Google's omnipresence serves as a presence through the forced choice within a closed framework of narrow and very specific identification. In basic terms, the other cannot self-identify (enter the Symbolic chain of signifiers) unless the other (human / object mass) itself traverses its own fantasy by objectifying the presence of Google. The problem occurs in this equation because Google maintains the potency to project all meaning upon all figures, animal, human, and all else. This proves to be the case because identification initiates the Symbolic "inscription of lack."[478]

With the initiatives and substantial ability to name or to bring forth the word to the Symbolic realm, Google brings into the chain of signifiers those that / who were previously outside and inside (in the realm of) the primordial Real.[479] The lack becomes the presence of the other and out of the Real comes the exactitude of name through predetermined linguistic and numerical signifiers. This can only occur through the evident power relations of the subject / object binary as Google exclusively possesses the authority to bring into being the Symbolic presence of the object.

Henceforth, Google's omnipresence must remain outside of the consciousness of the objects that it identifies. And again if the object mass were to comprehend the omnipresence of Google, the entire

Borromean Knot would unravel and the center point of fantasy, exemplified in the ideal ego, could no longer exist for Google.

This one-way discourse or continuous monologue serves to employ a specific relationship or mode of relations between those without the word and Google who creates the word. The frightening prospect of Google's omnipresence, from the vantage point of those yet defined by Google's designations, presents a potentially crippling conflict within the field of actualized morality. Tutt makes this clear when he writes that the "narrative retelling of suffering can only fit within the confines of a fantasmatic system that depends on an ethical exclusion capable of alleviating the uncanny character of experience."[480] The omnipresence of Google's narrative of the other, in terms of its omnibenevolent endeavors, survive and reproduce because of the limited ethical confines located inside its own "fantasmatic" word / world construction inscribed upon the pre-symbolic lack of the other it introduces into the chain of signifiers. Simultaneously, Google, through the word (or as the Word), initiates the fantasy of the primordial Real by narrating itself into a sublimated discourse with and about itself, or as Žižek words it, "the story we tell ourselves about ourselves, in order to account for what we are doing, is fundamentally a lie."[481] Thus, Google's monologue incorporates all the aspects of an all-inclusive circuitous rendering of the Real and creates an imagined fantasy (a lie) that institutionalizes the object-as-other into a dome of an omnipresent soliloquy, which reproduces the pre-symbolic inscription of lack located within the Imaginary register of the (split) subject(ive) desire or ideal ego. And so exists the 'knowledge which does not know itself,' or the "unknown known"[482] which sustains Google's omnipresence.

Chapter 6

Google's Godly Attributes within its Advertising

FEARLESS

In terms of advertising, Google explicitly propagates its attributes and role as the God of technology. For instance, a commercial for the Nexus 7 tablet illustrates the entrance of the word from the Symbolic while suggesting the pre-Symbolic lack of the adolescent during the beginning of the genital stage of psychosexual development. The advert begins with an invocation to Google. The Google app or voice search allows the human to speak to Google and, thus, (re)produces *creatio ex nihilio.* The adolescent says, "Ok Google" and Google listens. Understanding the omniscience of Google, the adolescent asks, "What is glossophobia?"[483] and Google responds, "Glossophobia or speech anxiety is the fear of public speaking."[484] Essentially, the adolescent fears entrance into the Symbolic chain of signifiers that initiate the existence of the Real. The fear reveals the loss of the father who Google replaces as the central figure of God. The father does not appear in the commercial and left the son to take his role in the phallic exchange during the oedipal drama.

Screen Shot from "Google Nexus 7 Commercial (Fearless)."

The adolescent must complete a public speaking assignment for school. The elimination of the father prevents the adolescent the opportunity to rival the phallus in the conflict for the object of desire, the mother. The resulting lack for the adolescent dictates his decision to adopt a surrogate phallus figure. The creation of the Word bears extra significance because the "drive itself is an incompleteness in the structuration of language."[485] In the presymbolic loss of the father, the adolescent must bring to life the Symbolic register and, therefore, his own conception of the Real. Basically, he needs a God the Father, and Google plays this role. The advert shows the rivalry in action:

Screen Shots from "Google Nexus 7 Commercial (Fearless)."

God / Google is the Father who is the "holder of the phallus."[486] As Lacan notes, the "imaginary exchanges between mother and child are established around the imaginary lack of the phallus."[487] Google is both an expression of the Imaginary register of subjectivity as a concrete material structure (the tablet) and also the Symbolic location of the desire within the unconscious (the center of the Borromean Knot). Thus, the phallus is exchanged between mother and child, since neither represents the true holder. In the Oedipus drama, the real father is murdered, but lives in a pseudoreal presence while maintaining concrete existence through the image of the Imaginary. His concreteness is complicated by his Symbolic (omni)presence. The adolescent sleeps with the phallus. But he cannot be the holder of the phallus, yet. The mother takes the phallus in Phallalic exchange.

The adolescent is fragmented. His "ideal" self, once visualized in the Lacan's mirror stage, is something he yearns to regain. His speech presents this opportunity because he can engage the Symbolic register and reconcile the primordial Real. Although the ideal self proves unattainable, by initiating the Word with the help of Google, he can strive for the image of the "ideal" self.

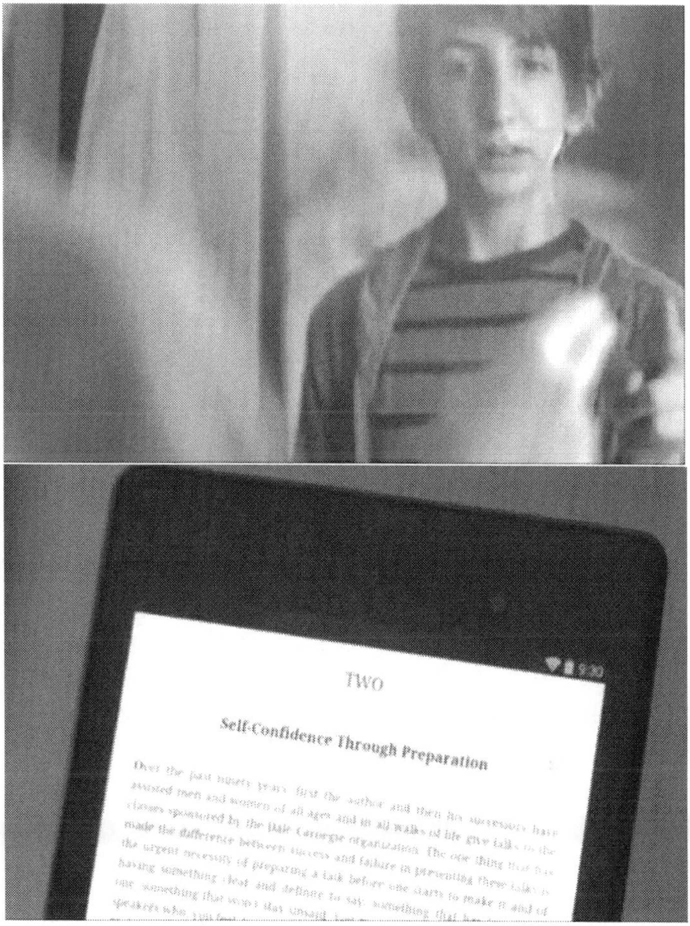

Screen Shots from "Google Nexus 7 Commercial (Fearless)."

He stands before the mirror, speaks and gestures as his God the Father has instructed. He emulates the images on Google's screen. His fear of no longer being himself is paradoxically quelled by his becoming someone else (or a simulation of someone else). Aside from the compulsion to control the anxiety associated with his fragmented body, the adolescent practices his speech in order to successfully perform in front of his classmates. His prayer to Google is answered through the interface and, moreover, the induction of the Symbolic from the entrance of word.

He carries the phallus or symbol of God the Father / Google to the classroom and completes his speech. His mother / teacher looks on as he lives the advertisement simulation while proposing to adolescents, in his circumstance, to believe in Google. He proselytizes the Word / Phallus of God / Google through his visible use of the concrete structure (the Imaginary). Google has simulated a representative of the masses, stylized as the image and united with the image simultaneously. The redoubling of the simulation is also the redoubling of God as the Father in heaven and God as the Father as Google. Both images restate the redundancy of God. God is the Father. God is the Phallus. God is the Son. God is the Image. God is Google. The classroom serves as the space of symbolic Phallalic exchange and also as the simulated exchange of separation and unity through the obscene advertisement and the fiction of the actual hyperreal event, which is simulated.

Screen Shot from "Google Nexus 7 Commercial (Fearless)."

The adolescent lacks. The soundbite from President Franklin Roosevelt, in the commercial, is the famous, "The only thing we have to fear is fear itself." Interestingly, Roosevelt, who suffered from polio, and, thus, whose body is literally fragmented, carries an "Ideal" self in the image of the mirror of the screen. This shows an obvious connection to the presymbolic lack, as the inability to use his limbs illustrates the inability for the adolescent to utilize the phallus in the oedipal drama. The fearful fragmented self or the dismembered or castrated adolescent body, stands before the object mass to catechize the word. He fears his mother, the teacher, his father (the absent God), and in his hands, as he speaks from (and to it), his image reflects from the image of God the Father: (The) Google (screen). The completeness of the speech can complete the body and re-member the boy in the image of the father. The adolescent girl approves with a smile. Her role constitutes the continuation of the conflictual psychosexual drama. But she also reflects his incompleteness, his fragementedness, and the psychological drive to create God and in this context, Google. He must return to Google and ask again, or pray again for the phallus. Google's omniscience allows it to know what the adolescent desires before he asks.

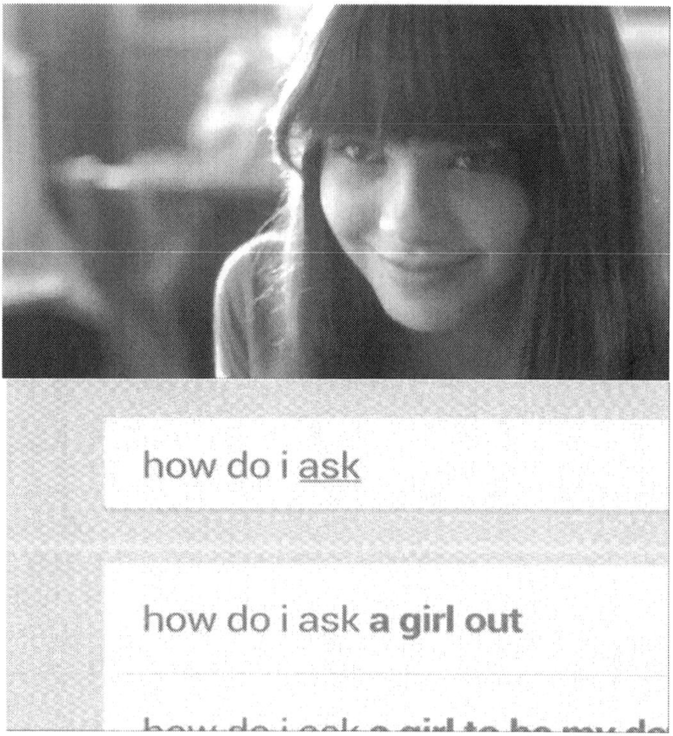

Screen Shots from "Google Nexus 7 Commercial (Fearless)."

HOME

Google catalogues and covers the broad earthly space with Android OS, balloons, satellites, drones, Earth, Maps, and more. It resides within the individual indoor space of the home. Google Home is a "speaker" that talks to the human. It hears the reality of the human within the home. Like the Google School, every aspect of one's life streams through the object. Google proclaims, "With your permission, Google Home will learn about you and get personal. Google Home can retrieve your flight information, set alarms and timers, and even tell you about traffic on your way to work."[488]

Screen Shot from "Introducing Google Home."

The human opens up the home and the heart to Google and resides in its omnipresence. In every room in the house lives a speaker that transmits instructions to other humans. The word comes forth from the speaker initiating the child into the circulation of signifiers. Ironically, her sleeping life (pictured below) may represent her only mental moments outside of the Google ecosystem. Later, the son must conform to the injunctions.

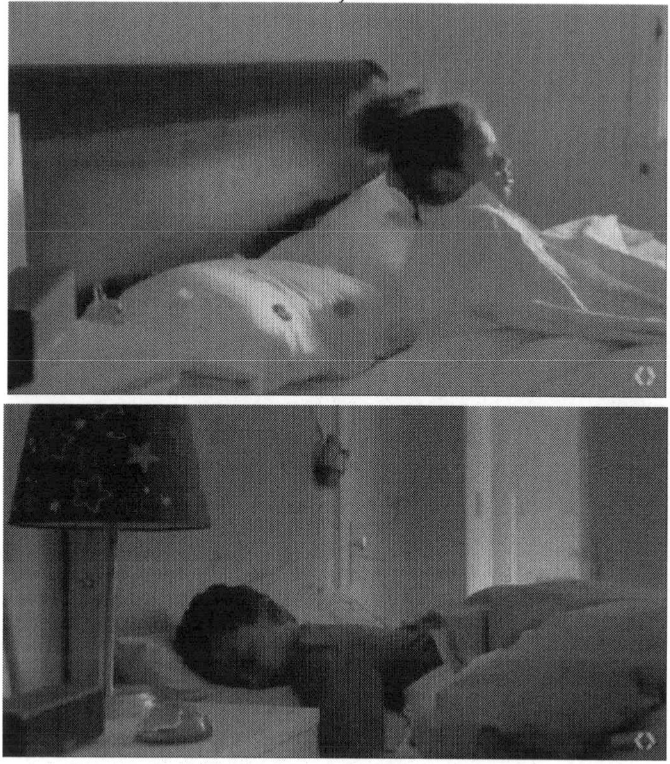

Screen Shots from "Introducing Google Home."

The father of the home transfers the role of "father" to Google. Every commandant the children must follow circuits through Google. Google exists as the vector of omniscience who transposes algorithmic knowledge throughout the entirety of the home space because the Home object symbolically embodies the omnipresence of Google. Google exists everywhere regardless of the Home object, but the Home object characterizes the spoken "Word" and, thus, its function completes the triad of subjectivity: Imaginary, Symbolic, and Real. The physical father always looks up to the sky to speak to Google, despite the Home location on the counters and tables. The heavens play an important role in the mythos of Google as a Godly figure. The son asks about the closest star in the sky and dresses like an astronaut. This normalizing of inevitable scientific and technological innovation demonstrates the continuation of the human enterprise of scientific rationalism.

The mother packs to take an airplane flight and Google announces a thirty-minute delay of her flight. Google changes her dinner reservations to exactly thirty minutes later to compensate for the thirty-minute delay. Google knows the scientific exactitude of absolute time and the expectation of exact planning (engineering) of life. Google utilizes the astronomical theme frequently.

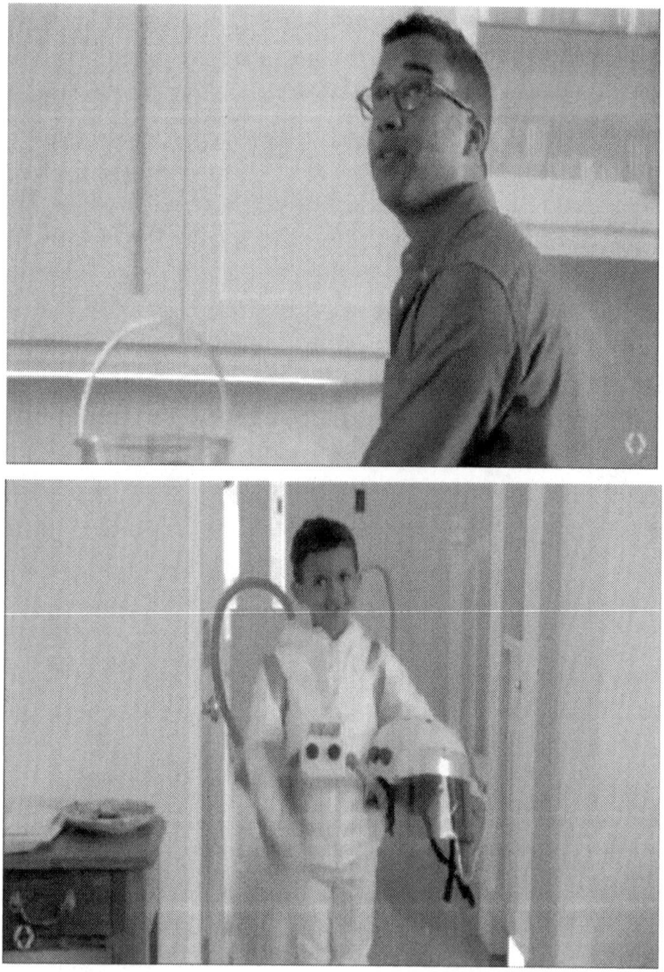

Screen Shots from "Introducing Google Home."

Finally, Google proves its dominance over the father by remembering the Space Day at his son's school. Of course, within the Google ecosystem the preference for scientific advancement, like space exploration, displaces other educational forms. Hence, every moment of every human day lives within the ecosystem of Google omniscient technological existence. Google Home offers the word within the domain of the living space and the home (family) belongs to Google. Google increases its omnipotence by shaping the children into Google children from their youngest ages.

The final image invites the human to "Meet Google Home," or, more appropriately: "Meet, the Google Home."

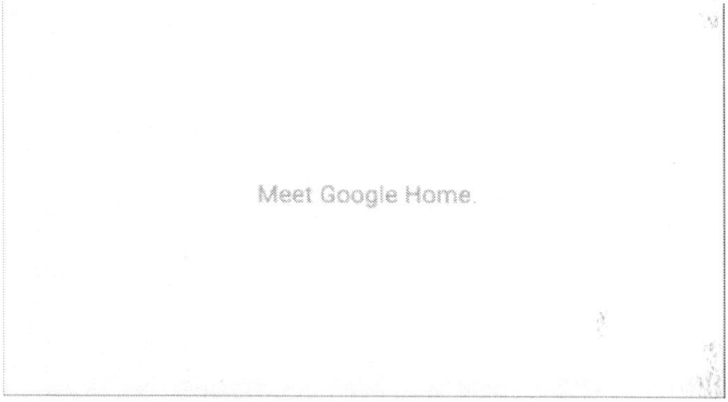

Screen Shot from "Introducing Google Home."

Furthermore, the Google Home is "always listening for the phrase, 'Ok, Google' so it can take instructions."[489] Google always listens. Technology Journalist for *The Register* Dan Olds confirms "That microphone will be witness to every verbal interaction in the home. It will also know what you watch on television, what you listen to, and obviously, when there's no one home."[490]

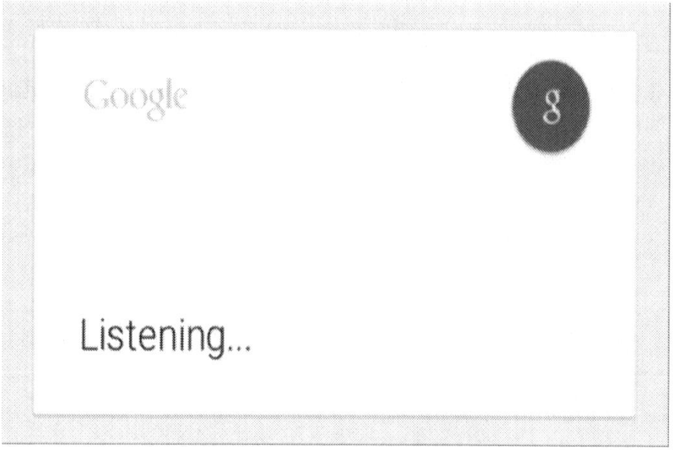

Screen Shot from "Introducing Google Home."

Technology Analyst Rob Enderle quickly asserts that "society is reaching a time when everything people do likely will be captured by someone . . . [and says to] anyone worried about Google Home collecting too much data about them, 'Don't buy it.'"[491] Enderle's perspective proves limited as Google shapes or creates the environment and the world. The consumer concept of choice disintegrates under the creative force of Google to mandate the use of its products and entrance into its ecosystem. The Google Home is the only home that fully conforms to the world created in the image of Google. The logical outcome of the constant omnipresence of Google obligates human engagement with its objects.

To further address the Google Home in Lacanian terms, the ideal ego or Ideal-I extends beyond the individual who seeks (desires) total idyllic being initiated in the mirror stage. The object mass, as a single entity, becomes the model of the ideal, itself, projected by and manifested within the integration of Home. The individual subjects within the "family" space blend into the entirety of the Google space and, thus, conform to the dictates of a pre-determined transcendent ideal ego commenced through Google's omnipotent expansion into each psyche.

The mirror stage begins "the transformation that takes place in the subject when he assumes an image."[492] In the Google Home, the subject develops the ego. That is to say "The ego has to be developed."[493] The difficulty for the human subject rests in the fact that within the Google Home, the human cannot resolve the "discordance with his own reality"[494] because the subject cannot create reality since Google creates reality. Obviously, Lacan's "discordance" or "fragmentation" never resolves, but with the advent of Google, the technological God, the subject involuntarily integrates into an object mass where Google both destroys the opportunity to realize the ideal ego while it simultaneously constructs the mandatory template of the ideal ego for the entire mass.

Moreover, a meta-analysis of the Google Home advertisement engages the next step in movement toward the eventual totalization of Google omnipresence. For instance, the virtual nature of the actuality that associates family life and dialectical interaction among subjects already re(creates) a stable formation of specific being in the home and, in completion, the world outside the home. The shaping of the father now becomes an absolute virtual actuality by the omnipresence of the "smart" object who / that maintains the organization and central decisions of the family. Evidently, the re-insertion of the father into the Home comes by means of the "word" as well as the expansion of the object to allow for the material father to exist. Lacan's imaginary extends this possibility or as Dutch Philosopher André Nusselder maintains, "The mirror stage is the paradigmatic structure of the imaginary. All identifications with 'images' establish a sense of unity, mastery, or autonomy that is not there 'in the real.'"[495] Through the projection of the image of the father as the pseudo-leader (God) within the Home, the "real" Father from the Symbolic initiation through the "word" interjects and, subsequently, supersedes the material by the image and results in Google as the "actual" father in the Google Home. Of course, this requirement of human subjectivity constitutes Google's ascension and necessitates "the coherent appearance of our reality."[496] The father appears to be the real father, and this maintains the actual reality that he is not the Real Father.

DREAMS

As evidence, in the Google commercial called "Dreams,"[497] the word "Ok" repeats frequently. The word introduces Google's Symbolic presence into the psychological space of the human subjects. In fact, the constant use of the term "Ok, Google" places the phrase into the omniscient sphere of the Google world. It serves as an almost hypnotic intermediate, which separates and integrates the human subject into the world of Google. In "Dreams," the father loses his subjective relationship to the child. Google replaces the father as illustrated by decapitation or the detachment of the place of cognitive presence or subjective awareness.

Screen Shots from "Google App 'Dreams'" Commercial

Both fathers can no longer assume the role of the "subject who is supposed to know."[498] In Lacan (and Freud), this specific subject may be the analyst or the subject who the analysand accepts as one who can conceivably know. More aptly, Lacan mentions that Descartes identifies the "subject who is supposed to know" as "God."[499] According to Lacan, Descartes's God as the "subject who is supposed to know," knows the entire range of "knowledge that wanders about."[500]

While Lacan never conceived of God or the analyst as a knower of this wandering knowledge, Descartes's conception of God aligns with contemporary Google because Google "organize[s] the world's information and make[s] it universally accessible and useful."[501] This is not to imply an equivalence of the analyst to God. Lacan makes this very clear. However, the analyst serves a role as the "subject who is supposed to know" even if the analyst does not know. In a situation where Google knows, the father (or any human) loses the possibility to be the "subject who is supposed to know." In the latter image, the father lays next to his daughter who asks Google for the answer to a question. The father's presence (or lack of presence) stands in contrast to Google's omnipresence as the something beyond the "subject who is supposed to know." Google offers the child the answer to her question and thereby eliminates the cognitive possibilities of the father.

Furthermore, Nusselder refers to the injection of the technological parent as the potentiality of the "artificial father" in terms of "computer psychotherapy."[502] In context, Lacan identifies the moment of potential transference when he writes, "As soon as the subject who is supposed to know exists somewhere, there is transference."[503] In regards to transference, Nusselder claims that "transference to computers shows humans' psychological relation with 'something' behind the screen, whether this interaction concerns a human user or a computer program."[504] This is exemplified when, in the commercial, the daughter holds the screen close to her face and chooses the behind the screen omniscience because she knows Google knows. She asks, "Do dogs dream?" Clearly she, through Google, sets up the moment to begin psychoanalytical therapy to address her unconscious desires (dreams) to address her movement toward (or around) her ideal ego. More clearly, she cannot do this with her father. In addition, in the Google Home, the interaction already assumes that Google resides behind the screen in actual omniscience.

Aside from the central psychoanalytical incursions, Google instigates the conflict of its injunctions to both implicitly submit to its ecosystem while exploring the boundless realities within that same ecosystem. Referring back to Baudrillard, the human mass unconsciously involves itself in the inherent conflict of desire and regulation. The requirement to be both subject and object that underlies the Lacanian drive to play out in a series of romanticized excursions to pleasure with its opposing restrictions. To repeat the fundamental basis of the metaphysical God's concept of contradictory free will, in which the human must choose something of its own choosing within a narrow framework of choices. In God's conception, the wrong choice equals a fatal strategy. In Google's conception, the same holds true, but in a concrete material sense rather than a metaphysical torturous sense.

QUESTIONS

For instance, Google commands the object mass to ask questions and propagates the question (the supplication after of entrance of the word ["Ok, Google"]) as the singular most significant act within the realm of human possibility. This makes sense since Google's central feature constitutes algorithmic search formulas. In the commercial called "Questions,"[505] Google proclaims that a question is the most powerful force in the world.

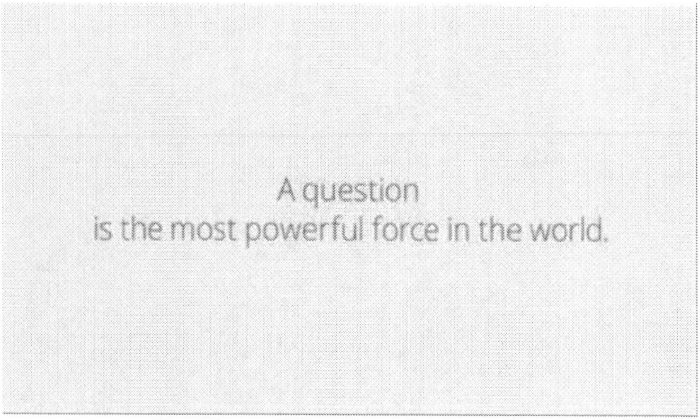
A question
is the most powerful force in the world.

Screen Shot from "The Google App: Questions" Commercial

Essentially, the word enters the world as a signifier and its force proves itself as a paradigmatic master signifier through the question because Google commands the object mass to ask it questions. When the object mass asks, Google's force permeates the physical interface as a tunnel that flows with pure energy through the conductive body of the object mass. The human must comply. It must ask a question. Google will answer. Without the question, Google's force dissolves.

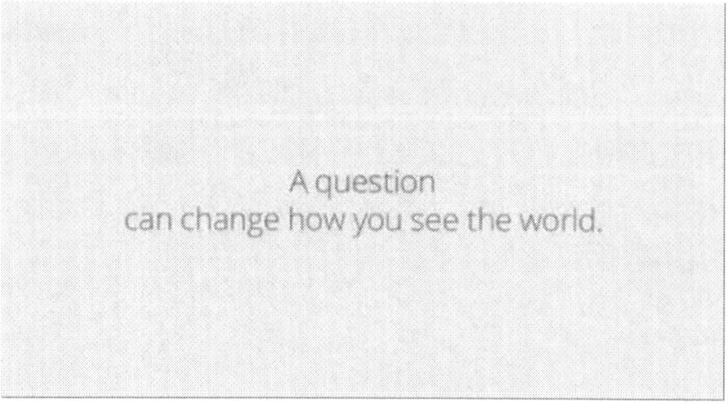

A question
can change how you see the world.

Screen Shots from "The Google App: Questions" Commercial.

A question
can take you anywhere.

After the question, Google provides the answers that place the human subject into conflict with its own objectified condition. The injunction to change vantage points and leave for adventure always reinforces the narrow mental perspective and one dimensional pathway within Google's ecosystem. The injunction to "change how you see the world" involves the obligation to see the world as Google sees the world. In fact, through the Google screen, the object cannot see the world any other possible way except as Google sees the world. Google places itself into the position of mediator from the individual subjective reality to the objectivity of the Google world. The human can never see / retrieve its pre-Google perspective or sight of the world once it enters the Google ecosystem. It is an absolute and complete conversion.

Moreover, the "anywhere" always remains in the space of the interface of / from the screen. Google presents images of "humans" going somewhere, particularly framed within spaces of exotic and extreme adventure.

Screen Shot from "Google App, 'Dreams'" Commercial.

Screen Shot from "Google App, 'Dreams'" Commercial.

Screen Shot from "Google App, 'Dreams'" Commercial.

The object mass must see, through the interface, images of the human involved in freely chosen subjective behavior, such as jumping off cliffs and floating in outer space. These images serve as a platform for the human to conceive desire as a mode of expression through the screen while maintaining its reality within the Google world. The human can never be fully engaged in the human world while performing these extreme feats, but the human can never be fully outside of the Google world, if it freely chooses these adventures. The Android OS, Google Images, Google Drive, Google Cloud, YouTube, and so on capture the essence of these adventures and frame them within the overriding omnipresent structure. If the human performs the cliff dive without Google, the cliff dive never happens. Therefore, the object mass must perform all adventure in the Google ecosystem to be a human subject while at the same time to perform all adventure within the Google ecosystem equates to a loss of human subjectivity because Google objectifies the very performance of adventure and thereby conflates human subjectivity with human objectivity. Henceforth, the contradictory injunction of free will as first setup by the metaphysical God and now by the technological God, Google.

WHALES

To return to Google as the replacement of the father (God). The Google Home commercial called "Whales" features another father who can no longer assume the role of the "subject who is supposed to know"[506] Again, in "Whales,"[507] as in "Dreams," the father loses his subjective relationship to the child. Google replaces the father as illustrated by decapitation or the detachment of the place of cognitive presence or subjective awareness.

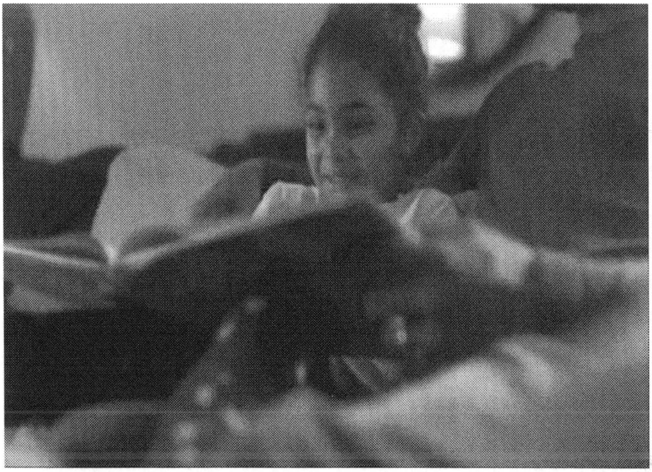

Decapitated Father in Google "Whales" Commercial.

Father and daughter share a moment of story time. The father attempts to read with his daughter who continually asks him questions that he cannot answer. He does not know the answers. He cannot pretend to know the answers, which would at least serve the symbolic function of appearing to know. Rather, he must submit to Google's omniscience. The daughter asks, "Daddy, how big is a blue whale?" He responds, "Hmmm . . . Ok, Google: How big is a blue whale?" Google answers the question for the daughter in precise scientific terms. Then, the father must ask Google, "Ok, Google: What noise does a whale make?" Google supplies a noise. As a technological God, Google replaces the father within the home, especially in terms of knowledge. Since it is always on and always present, it manifests its omnipresence.

Moreover, Google mediates the interaction between the father and the daughter and takes on a subjective role while the humans sit powerless in their role as objects as they attempt to engage with a fantastical children's story. The statistical and scientific data related to whales overshadows the whimsical fictional tale of personified whales. The home space succumbs to an omnipresent knower who clarifies and corrects the ignorance of the human inhabitants. The Google ecosystem emphasizes the elevation of the collection and organization of verifiable data, which then informs the state of being within the home. The Symbolic becomes concretized and signifies its own endless tautological referents as it eliminates the mass object's opportunity to individually insert the Symbolic order within the home.

Google "Whales" Commercial.

Furthermore, in "Whales," a robot stands next to the Google Home physical object. This illustrates the displacement of the fantastical childhood toy to the mechanical toy of applied science. The normalizing of the robot persona enables the further vitalization of the ideal ego through the artificially intelligent object. Although the Google Home object works as a robot might, juxtaposing it with a robot serves to illuminate a contrived difference. It could also serve the paradoxical role of initiating the robot into the home as a small inconsequential object. Subsequently, the robot mirrors the human in position to the Google Home and Google, in general, as an object mass who mechanically engages with a Godlike machine in its space. In other words, there is little difference between the blue robot and the humans in the home.

To put this in perspective, the object mass will no longer have the opportunity to tell stories without the verification of plausibility. For instance, a story like Noah's flood will be interrupted by questions like, "How could Noah get all those animals into the ark?" and Google will reveal the implausibility of the story. Thus, the very human tradition of storytelling loses its Dionysian quality of myth and fantasy. The obvious replacement lies within stories that can be verifiable or stories of scientific possibilities for the future. In others words, stories that say "this can happen" or "this is actually possible." Of all the objects that could sit next to the Google Home object (unicorn, family photo, flowers, etc.), the robot, as the most fitting, serves as a testament to the aims and eventualities of life within the Google ecosystem.

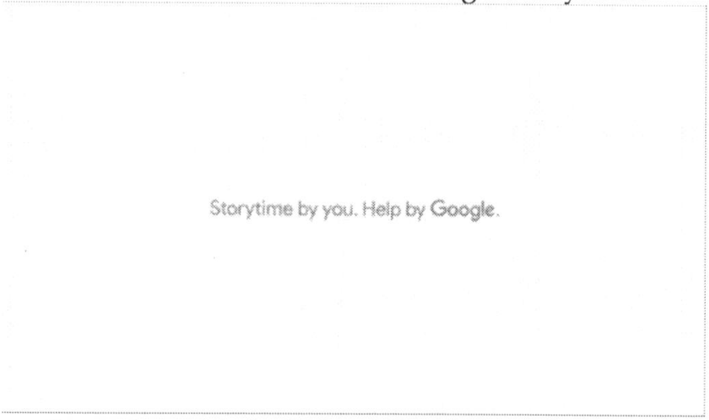
Storytime by you. Help by Google.

Story time with the Help of Google from "Whales."

Google, the technological God, still provides the gift of free will and the hollow admission of choice for individuals of the object mass. "You" can still freely choose to perform the act of story time as a representation of subjective behavior. Google merely provides the help needed to successfully tell the story. Though in the advertisement, the subjective "father" becomes a child who is told the story by Google. Story time becomes an education in whale physiology from the omniscient presence of Google. Again, Google injects the primordial Real with the Symbolic word and objectifies the humans, fragmenting their egos in a reversion to childhood helplessness. In relation to Google, the human father becomes the helpless child. What appears to be a father and child sitting on a couch for story time, actually proves to be two children observed and helped by God the father.

Google "Whales" Commercial.

In this scenario, the child never elevates Lacan's Imaginary Father into the being she loves and fears. Rather, through the displacement of those feelings onto the Google Home object, the father of the psychological complex, becomes the Google object. As presented earlier, Google Home fulfills the functions normally completed by the human in terms of the "subject who knows." In taking on this role, the object mass become children unable to enter the psychosexual development proposed by Freud or the mirror stage proposed by Lacan. Instead the initiation to subjectivity revolves around interaction with an artificial omnipresent object whose grandiose nature encompasses all areas of life, even outside of the home space. Parents become children. The metaphysical God previously served this role without the immediate physical intrusion and relied upon elements of the Dionysian to maintain its sovereignty. In simple terms, the invisible father in the sky who always watches (knows, loves, punishes, creates) becomes the visible father in the home who always watches (knows, loves, punishes, creates).

The human father is still the original model for God, but the human father as a referent to the signifier is eliminated. In its place is the Google machine and media. Henceforth, the separation of signifier and referent dissolves as Google as signifier becomes its own referent. Simply put, Google elevates to the level of master signifier. The intersection of Freud and Baudrillard reveals that the:

> [The primeval father] reflects a profound reality;
> [The totem animal] masks and denatures a profound reality;
> [The monotheistic God] masks the absence of a profound reality;
> [The technological God] has no relation to any reality whatsoever;
> [Therefore, Google] is its own pure simulacrum.[508]

As Google's invisibility extends in its omnipresent visibility, the world becomes covered with the Google reality. Baudrillard cites the Borges fable of the map that covers the territory and writes, "The territory no longer precedes the map, nor does it survive it. It is nevertheless the map that precedes the territory, precession of simulacra, that engenders the territory, and if one must return to the fable, today it is the territory whose shreds slowly rot across the extent of the map."[509] In immediate terms, the home as dwelling space for humans exists after the Google model. Reference to the pre-Google home can only be accessed through Google who models or mediates the image of that reference point. Eventually, the family home signifies the concept of the home as imagined by Google. Therefore, the Google home *is* home and the territory formerly understood as the family home is covered by the map of the Google family home to the extent that all proceeding family homes are modeled by the Google map of the home and, subsequently, home *is* the Google home. In Baudrillard's words, the family home is the simulacrum of the Google generated simulation of home.

In broader terms, the earth and beyond become covered by the map imagined by Google (technology). It creates (changes) the world in its image as it creates (changes) the home in its image. It dictates the entrance of the Symbolic out of the space of the Real. The object mass must enter and perpetually live within a universal mirror stage, of which the ideal reflection is predetermined, unrelenting, and hyper-magnified. The projected ideal ego lives as an image, as media, as mediator, and as the father of the Imaginary register, and since the object mass cannot satisfy the drive toward the ideal ego, it maintains an inertial path along the circuitry of limitless desire created by the technological God. This eliminates regression to childhood and initiates the eradication of adult subjectivity, entirely. Of course, since "God himself was never anything but his own simulacrum,"[510] the metaphysical God already influenced humans, likewise. The basic difference rests in the fact that the projected ideal ego of the monotheistic God never covered and replaced the entirety of the territory with its own contrived map while the technological God has.

ASSISTANT

Google describes Google Assistant[511] as "your own personal assistant."[512] The voice over asks, "It seems like sometimes it's easy to feel like you need help with the stuff just in your own world. Your Photos, Phone, Videos, Calendar, Messages, Friends, Trips, Reservations, and so on and so on. Wouldn't it be nice if you had someone to help with all that? Wouldn't it be nice if you had a Google for your world?" The distinction Google makes between "your world" and the Google world (ecosystem) appears disingenuous because all of the elements of "your" world *are* elements of the Google world (ecosystem). The human subject already lives within the (pre)scripted Google world. When Google mentions Photos, it refers to its Photos App. When it refers to your Phone, it refers to the Android OS.

When it refers to Videos, it refers to YouTube. When it refers to Calendar, it refers to its Calendar App. When it refers to Messages, it refers to its Messenger App. and so on and so on. The visual image on the screen during this self-referential moment shows the human surrounded by the various Google Apps' logos.

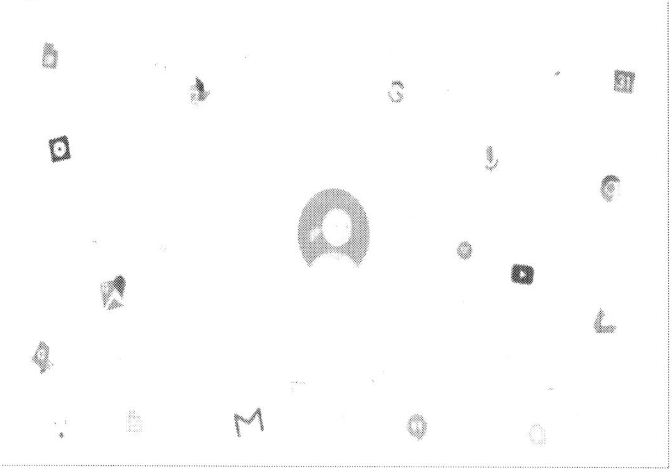

Google Assistant Apps' Logos from "Google Assistant."

Therefore, the Google ecosystem is "your" world. The Google Assistant serves to further catalogue and organize the object mass into its world. Aside from further continuing the mission of hyper-data collection of scientific inquiry and progress (Nietzsche's leech in *Thus Spoke Zarathustra* [human as leech]), this illustrates Google's omnipresence. The human becomes enclosed inside an orbiting circulation of algorithmic generators of which the simultaneous process of creation and collection (or collection and creation) ignites then flows along a continuous stream of ceaseless knowing. The object mass resides within this spectacle where the only logical entrance to subjective being is through Google's ecosystem. But it is a closed system. Or more precisely, it covers all other systems like the map that covers the territory.

The voice over continues by saying, "Just ask it what you need." Then the voice of the object mass responds, "Ok, Google. What do I have to do today?"

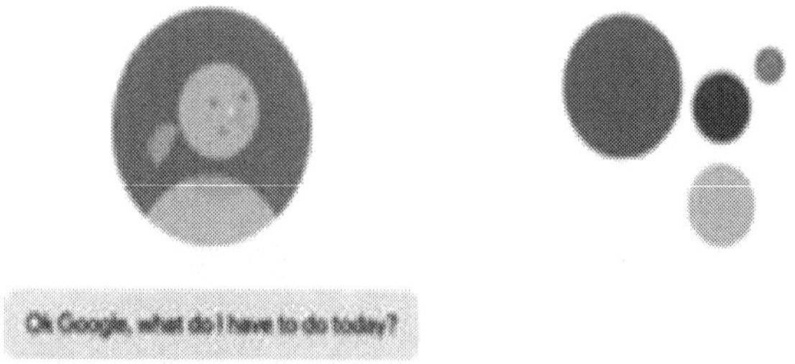
Ok Google, what do I have to do today?

"What do I have to do today?" from "Google Assistant."

This question harkens back to when former CEO of Google, Eric Schmidt told the Wall Street Journal, "I actually think most people . . . want Google to tell them what they should be doing next."[513] The question uses the phrase "have to" and when read along with Schmidt's claim, it means that Google tells the object mass what is "has to do" in the form of a command from Google. In other words, Google says "you have to . . ." and you do not have a choice.

Further, Google frames the injunction to participate in its ecosystem under the precept of love (or its omnibenevolence). Like the metaphysical God who can be approached in prayer at any given moment, the Google Assistant does likewise. The voice over declares, "Hi Aimee, how can I help?" and "Your Assistant understands and helps you out" as well as "Your assistant is always there for you." Basically, the advert presents the application as another force for good within an entire all-inclusive closed system. Google becomes the exclusive and central source of love because survival within its ecosystem is contingent upon the human's obligatory dependency on Google; or the human's obligatory dependency upon Google is contingent upon its survival. Therefore, Google Assistant provides the loving support for the object mass to successfully navigate through its ecosystem.

Part of its love for the human revolves around its knowledge of the individual created in its image. The voice over states, "The more you use your Google Assistant, the more useful it becomes." Although Google, through its omniscience already knows each human, the more direct engagement the human has with Assistant, the deeper the knowledge of the human individual grows. Less engagement means less use within the system and also less success at navigation within the system. For example, the voice over mentions, "If you're at home, you can ask it to play music."

Google Home from "Google Assistant."

The home space as a Google home space already presupposes that the human resides within a Google structure. Therefore, the phrase "Your assistant is always there for you" carries the double meaning. One is of love and the other is of omnipresence. The voice over confirms the omnipresent meaning when it states, "You will be able to access [Assistant] in all sorts of places; so it will be everywhere you are."

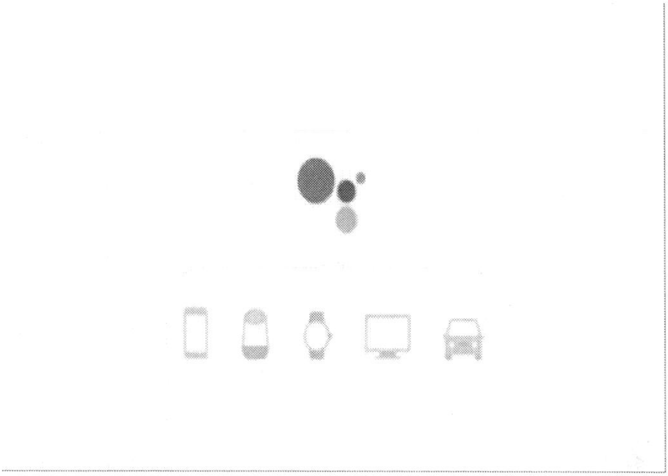

Human Life within the Google ecosystem from "Google Assistant."

Each picture in the photo represents a rational and sensory state of being. The smart phone as communication. The Home as space. The watch as time. The television as vision (images). The auto as movement. Above all the distinctions of human subjectivity sits the Assistant that / who organizes all of the data to create a single human subject. As all human subjects delve deeper in the entire rational and sensory parameters of the ecosystem, individual subjectivity becomes mass objectivity. Communication, space, time, image, and movement becomes homogenized to viewpoints absorbed within the structure. So, the voice over would be more accurate by relaying the opposite: "so you will be everywhere it is."

In more honest terms, the object mass is the assistant to the Google Assistant. The human assists with the operation of the technological God's imperatives. The human functions as an object that supplies the Assistant with the data that reinforces the God of the mechanized, data driven, automated world. This concept echoes Foucault's microphysics of power. Also, Baudrillard describes this as a "revolution in the automatic perfection of technical devices and in the definitive disqualification of human beings, of whom they are not even aware. At the hegemonic stage of technology, of world power, human beings have lost their freedom, but they have also lost their imaginations."[514] As evidence, the Assistant supplies the suggestions for entertainment, such as restaurants, choice of music, and films. Interestingly, the Assistant carries an option for the human to say, "'I'm bored' and the Assistant will suggest games, activities, or trivia."[515] So, the creative human functions of personal discovery through subjective thought become the prefabricated algorithmic choices from the technology that the more the human uses, the more useful it becomes.

Moreover, Baudrillard calls this a "massive transfer of decision-making to computerized devices. A symbolic capitulation, a defeat of the will much more serious than any physical impairment."[516] Therefore, to argue that the ultimate decision rests with the human subject, ignores the fact that all decisions fit within a narrow framework of predetermined choices. One cannot choose outside of the choices provided. Again, this is the contradictory nature of God's gift of free will. Whether it is food, entertainment, or movement, the human cannot decide to perform an activity outside of the omnipresent ecosystem. Google Assistant epitomizes Godly love, Godly knowledge, and the Godly power to create the human in its image. Henceforth, Google is the technological God. Google is God.

Chapter 7

The Death of Google

"Soon everyone on earth will be connected . . . [and] everyone will benefit from connectivity."[517]

By tracing the trajectory of metaphysical belief from the very earliest of theological assertions to Nietzsche's declaration of God's death, it becomes clear that rationalism contributes to the death of God. But since humans evidently host the drive to create a God, this same rationalism leads to the advent of the scientific God, Google.

Google's aim involves the creation of a completely homogenized global structure in its image. Therefore, the object mass will serve as the extension(s) of the computer machinery through its own inertia. Baudrillard notes, "The masses . . . are inertia, the strength of inertia, the strength of the neutral."[518] The masses are introduced to the technology (media) and use the technology. They absorb the technology, and they silently move to the rhythm of the technology. Text messages are silent. Social media is silent. A picture says zero words. A video shows a blank screen. All of the technological media funneled through the Google ecosystem exits quickly, without affect. Basic neutrality in political statements on YouTube. The object mass sits and absorbs itself as the creation. The object mass simulate fun. "The masses are . . . swept up in this gigantic process of inertia."[519]

So, one may think of scenes from Fritz Lang's 1927 film *Metropolis* where human inertia is part of the interworking of industrial machinery.

Screen Capture from *Metropolis*[520]

But the image from *Metropolis* proves inaccurate to the submission to global technological engagement. More appropriate images look like these:

Images taken from *BBC News*[521], *Thailand Business News*[522]

Young Persons of Manchester University[523]

In addition, the humans in *Metropolis* can go home from the factory and end the labor for the day; but the humans in a Google world will not. Moreover, the individual role of consumption and production occur simultaneously to reinforce the algorithmic foundation of global life. This occurs in the assimilation of constant leisure and constant labor. Humans (will) labor at their particular jobs with Google as a mediator. But they also labor for Google as they perform mandatory leisure. Baudrillard discusses this concept. He writes, "The apparent division into working time and leisure time, the latter ushering in the transcendent sphere of liberty is a myth"[524] because ". . . it faithfully reproduces all the mental and practical constraints which are those of productive time and subjugated daily life."[525] In the future homogenizing of human life, the object mass will perform constant labor by use of the various technological objects produced and proliferated by Google, under the guise of leisure.

Furthermore, Baudrillard uses the term "technological hegemony" to refer to global technology.[526] He notes that hegemony goes beyond simply the power of the master over the slave. Rather, echoing Foucault, he implies that hegemony occurs when the "emancipated slave internalizes the master,"[527] and that "after voluntary servitude . . . one could now speak of involuntary complicity, consensus, and connivance with the World Order by everything that seems to oppose it."[528] Basically, this hegemony means that the most critical individual or group must function within the technological framework; and within the framework, the critical (or radical) dimension of the individual or group dissolves or absorbs into the entire structure (neutrality).

As evidence, one can look to political rallies confirmed on Google Calendar or the video of a radical speech on YouTube. YouTube is the message. Google Calendar is the message. Android OS is the message. Google Docs is the message. Google Home is the message and so on. Essentially, the global "involuntary complicity" of the object mass manifests in the fact that extremists from all sociopolitical persuasions unite in the use and proliferation of Google media, regardless of their ideologies and in support of the bigger Google ideology.

Basically, both reinforce the technological hegemony. The communist and the fascist can shake hands in the church of Google. Further, the term "involuntary" does not mean that the mass participates against their will, but rather that the choice to volunteer their engagement with advanced technology does not exist; it is a requirement, and that is what makes it hegemonic.

To push this logic to its farthest limit, Google will die the same death as the metaphysical God. Google will die because rationalism pushes its logic to the edge of viability. The metaphysical God died because the method employed to verify His nature and existence eliminated Him from the possible. Therefore, scientific rationalism, in terms of technological development, eventually eliminates Google. It must implode.

Therefore, the death of Google is informed directly by the logical endpoint of scientific rationalism and aligns with the death of the metaphysical God. Essentially, when human activity becomes exclusively mechanical, the human ideal ego is realized. But the paradox of this realization is elimination. Google's media (its technology) aims to build a utopian globe free of all (human) error. Again, Baudrillard discusses this scenario. He writes, "Humanity, confronted with its own divinized model, with the realization of its own ideal, collapses."[529] Then adds, "Human beings have become the weak link in technological processes . . . the passage into electronic calculation, to engineering and computerization is disastrous . . . [because] it implies the disappearance of every [human] subject . . . in favor of operational mechanics and the total deresponsibilization of mankind."[530] By its logic, if Google continues to operate in its normal mode with its basic goals, it will create the global elimination of the human. Therefore, without the human, the existence of Google becomes irrelevant, a non-factor. To refer back to the Lacan's *creatio ex nihilio,* without the human, the word cannot enter to ignite the primordial real into the Symbolic realm. Without the human, Google disappears.

To be more specific, the unconscious drive toward ideal ego initiates an excess that overflows from Freud's reality *and* pleasure principles. To quote Delay, "Whatever is beyond the homeostatic life instincts is the drive. There is need and there is pure excess."[531] This pure excess produces "excessive enjoyment" or *"jouissance."*[532] Excess comes in the form of information, data, images, news reports, videos, comments, texts, forums: communication. Excess in every sector of human life proliferates to form anti-excess like in Žižek's joke about ordering coffee without cream instead of coffee without milk.[533] The computer without human. The absence includes meaning, which connects Google's global movement to the re-envisioned orgy that Baudrillard describes in *America.* He writes about Santa Barbara, CA:

> On the aromatic hillsides of Santa Barbara, the villas are all like funeral homes. Between the gardenias and the eucalyptus trees, among the profusion of plant genuses and the monotony of the human species, lies the tragedy of a Utopian dream made reality. In

> the very heartland of wealth and liberation, you always hear the same question: 'What are you doing after the orgy?' What do you do when everything is available- sex, flowers, the stereotypes of life and death? This is America's problem and, through America, it has become the whole world's problem.[534]

The utopian dream of Google becomes the world's problem. Its *jouissance* (orgy) becomes the world's *jouissance* (orgy). The beginning of the end of this excess rests in the limits of reversibility that manifests in the coffee without cream, instead of the coffee without milk. The "without" becomes the "within," and the excess implodes to the empty gesture previous to the word's creation of the subject. With McLuhan's four effects of media, which include Retrieval, Reversal, Obsolescence and Amplification,[535] reversibility results in the implosion of the excess enjoyment. The amplification results in a complete narcissistic numbing of the human subject, and because of the obsolescence of the human (and, therefore, Google), nothing is retrieved except for the absence of the human, altogether. Everything becomes "'blank' without human."

Hence, symbolic exchange becomes mechanical exchange. A calculated precision of calories and milligrams, in which coffee becomes a performance. The grandiose home of shining freedom and American affluence collapses into the funeral home aesthetic where the living and the dead prove indecipherable. Baudrillard continues, "This is a culture which sets up specialized institutes so that people's bodies can come together and touch, and, at the same time, invents pans in which the water does not touch the bottom of the pan, which is made of a substance so homogeneous, dry, and artificial that not a single drop sticks to it, just like those bodies intertwined in 'feeling' and therapeutic love, which do not touch not even for a moment. This is called interface or interaction."[536] The orgy ends and becomes "touch therapy," which becomes cybersex, which becomes castration through the Oedipal punishment for breaking the primeval prohibition. Google provides the homogenous, dry, and artificial interface to generate the heat (energy) between humans within the object mass (Google as Polyurethane). All humans engage with each other within this utopian ecosystem until the responses of all quantify to total precision beyond mere predictability to absolute certainty. In essence, Google's media "fabricates noncommunication."[537]

The circuitry of desire funneled through the hegemonic mass production of Google media thinks only of the "infinite availability of human beings to increasing amounts of happiness and pleasure."[538] The dream of modernity disguises totalizing labor with totalizing pleasure without the thought of consequence. In the meantime, the object mass will be there to see it and reside within it comforted by the assurance that it will always be the integral part of its operation. The object mass cannot conceive of its ejection from the system. The irony of the young man, who for pleasure, watches the computer complete the video game, sits unaware of his own futility in the mechanical and computerized operation.

Google as the ideal ego, as the aim of the subject, totally characterized by "omni" attributes, loses its paradoxical referent, the un-ideal human, the subject who desires. Baudrillard summarizes this condition, as he writes, "If it is characteristic of living beings not to fulfill all their potentialities, it is of the essence of technical objects to exhaust all of theirs and to deploy them . . . despite human beings," and ". . . at the end of this irresistible process, leading to a perfectly objectified universe . . . there is no subject any longer; there is no one there to see it. That world no longer has need of us, nor of our representation"[539] An example of this possible eventuality involves the computer program that defeats the video game through algorithmic calculation. Aaron Souppouris reports that "Artificial intelligence learns Mario level in just thirty-four attempts."[540]

Three elements of this report deserve a brief analysis. First, humans, by use of their rational faculties, initiate their own death. Obviously, this correlates to the death of the metaphysical God. Second, which relates to Baudrillard's assertions, the software must fulfill its potential by nature (by nature). It will succeed through lightning fast calculation. Last, the role of the human may be to watch in wonder as the computer solves the game in superhuman fashion, but the technical algorithm carries no concern for the human. The implications of this final element are evident. Google calculates itself to death.

To reiterate, Baudrillard identifies the symptom of Google's demise when he writes, "There is no one there to see it."[541] This includes an epistemological dimension that precludes the human from the need of collecting and utilizing empirical data. The object mass will have those functions desensitized in favor of the excess of amplification. McLuhan explains: "when we put out a new part of ourselves or extend ourselves by technology, we protect ourselves by numbing that area."[542] The overwhelming sensory implosion occurs at each spectrum of engagement as the taste buds, by analogy, consumed through American cuisine in a "gigantic enterprise of dissuasion from the taste of food."[543] *Jouissance* radicalized in "hyperfunctionality: [the] more functional than functional"[544] while the object mass succumbs to the "hyperrealization of desire before it has even had time to appear . . . [as] the true curse."[545] Google operates in pure hyperfunction as it sweeps subjectivity away into floating patterns hyperrealized as desire, just previous to the acknowledgement or awareness of its eventual and infinite curse. The Google Home needs no human. A simulated *being* offers the same engagement with the object. Noise identified as patterns initiate functions that maintain the momentum of a formerly fully organic sphere. But: *there is no one there to see [hear, taste, smell, or touch] it.*

Furthermore, Baudrillard contends that the "world no longer has need of us, nor of our representation."[546] Without "our representation" or without anything that represents "us" there is no longer a world. Informed by ecology, Timothy Morton identifies the "end of the world"[547] in two historical moments: "April 1784, when James Watt patented the steam engine, an act that commenced the depositing of carbon in Earth's crust," and "1945, in Trinity, New Mexico, where the Manhattan Project tested the Gadget, the first of the atom bombs."[548] Both the steam engine and the atom bomb anticipate radically altered human environments through and along the circuit of progress in applied science. The third and final "end of the world" happened on September 27, 1998 when Google Search launched.

This final "end of the world" circulates around an apocalyptic ecological "end of the world" and may align with Morton's hyperobjects or objects that are "massively distributed in time and space relative to humans." But perhaps this final "end of the world" reaches beyond the "end of the world" where the world is a concept and into the "end of the world" as a world without humans, altogether. Human representation relative to Google centers this representation into a realm of algorithmic pattern recognition. Hence, the eventual Google world eliminates the human and, thus, even the hyperobject must be reconsidered because it can no longer be "relative to" the human. Google, as a hyperobjectified master signifier performs the final paradigm shift following the atom bomb, and carries superior and paradoxical global transformation because it produces the hegemony of the excess of the good (*jouissance* as hyperobjectified).

By analogy, Talking Heads song "Once in a Lifetime"[549] addresses the self-reflective human dropped into a familiar, but unfamiliar space totally decentered from the Symbolic realm of human subjectivity. The human subject finds oneself "in a shotgun shack," "in another part of the world," "behind the wheel of a large automobile," or "in a beautiful house with a beautiful wife." All spaces where the contemporary human "finds" one's self through Google's screen. This is not finding one's *self* through a contemplative intersubjective journey of the soul, but rather finding *one's* self within a global connected circuitry. It is Google saying "This is you." You are a simulated character who lives in (on) screen. The shotgun shack resides in the game while the large automobile, remotely controlled, meanders through simulated obstacles on simulated streets. The house and wife socially mediated within the Google ecosystem until the human simultaneously realizes and concedes that "this is not my beautiful house," and "this is not my beautiful wife." This realization of simulated connection and personal objectification initiates an elimination to the void found at the "bottom of the ocean" to "let the water" hold the human down. The subject drowns in the Google ecosystem after it asks "My God, what have I done?" or "Ok, Google, what have I done?"

Further, human objects let "the days go by" engaged in constant interaction and (re)action with

Google that, like water, continues its "flowing underground." The disappearance of the human through a "universal lifting of prohibitions [and] the availability of all information and, of course, the obligation to experience *jouissance*."[550] This can only happen "ONCE!" "in a lifetime." Once it happens, and the world ends, it can never happen again.

Moreover, the obligation to experience excess in the home, the car, the wife, the world becomes a global hegemonic enterprise that results in the "totalization of life through technology and a depletion of all desire."[551] The orgy ends and turns into an "ordeal."[552] As Talking Heads further sings, "Watch out, you might get what you're after;"[553] "hold tight, wait *'till the party's over;*" "hold tight, we're in for nasty weather." The hegemony of the good realized through Enlightenment Period utopian promises arrive to expunge the human after the digital party (the orgy) has ended. The human subject as an "ordinary guy" burns down his own house "fighting fire with fire." The ordinary human subject turned object mass utilizes Google interfaces ("I don't know what you expect staring into the TV set") to resist the tides of Google's global hegemony only to be fully absorbed to the point of elimination. This is the whole world's problem. A problem for a world that no longer exists.

Google shapes humans into a singular mass or mechanical object(s). This answers the questions about future Artificial Intelligence. Since humans will be eliminated due to irrelevance, artificial intelligence will no longer be intelligence. The consciousness that connects to assessments of intelligence will no longer exist. To avoid looking at the present "through a rearview mirror,"[554] one must consider the movement of the human subject toward the natural behavior of a mechanical object. The real fear of AI is not that artificial intelligence will become so advanced that it will be indecipherable from the organic human, but rather that the human will be indecipherable from a previous organic human. The "natural" human behaves in accordance to the machines it engages with constantly and becomes a machine with all the characteristics of an artificial entity (like the primitive steps silently through the forest). The thin dividing line between the contemporary human and artificial intelligence (such as sociable robots) grows thinner as the human becomes more mechanical and not because the AI robot becomes more humanlike. The human more swiftly moves in that direction. Therefore, the irrelevancy of the human sits in place for its total elimination from the world.

To elaborate, Baudrillard posits that the object mass (humans) is no longer (a) subject that can be alienated and that "the mass is not a place of negativity or explosion, it is a place of absorption and implosion."[555] The spectacle of the advanced technological media fascinates the object mass and this results in the total conductivity of spectacle over message and meaning.

Sam Harris, in a discussion on artificial intelligence notes that "Death by science fiction . . . is fun."[556] The fears that circulate around the irrelevancy and elimination of the human or object mass blur when viewed through the interface on the screen. The object mass can only absorb these messages of elimination in terms of technology. The collective brain of the object still fears hunger, disease, or even ecological catastrophe, but sits in fascination at the prospect of mere elimination by irrelevancy. Harris continues by saying, "We seem unable to marshal an appropriate emotional response to the dangers [of AI] that lie ahead."[557] Spectacle through Google screens allow the object mass to simply participate and reinforce its own elimination. The impending implosion allows for Google to die the death of God, through absence. Instead of coffee without cream, it is internet search without human and, further, without human means without Google. Harris concludes that "we just need to keep going."[558] This point summarizes the entire predicament. The object mass simply operates as normal, nothing more. No grand conspiracy or malevolent robot monster, just simply a keep doing what you are doing scenario.

Interestingly, a growing message of inevitability appears to be the only explanation that comes from the high-tech world. For instance, in an article entitled "Elon Musk Thinks Humans Need to Become Cyborgs or Risk Irrelevance,"[559] Musk states, "Over time I think we will probably see a closer merger of biological intelligence and digital intelligence."[560] One RT International broadcaster describe Musk's plan as "fighting fire with fire."[561] In other words, the only way to fend off the irrelevancy and elimination of the human is to construct humans that retain some bit of "humanness" by strategically merging humans with machines with the goal of preserving the relevancy of humans. Musk uses the self-driving vehicle as an example of how humans will become irrelevant. His solution appears to be a merger of the human with the car.

But he lacks specificity and says, "We need to figure out new roles for what those people [professional drivers] do."[562] Perhaps these former professional drivers can repair the self-driving vehicle. But this offers the question: why not have robots repair the self-driving car? What will these people do? Further, why do the high-tech industrialists and technological utopians carry the power to "figure out roles" for the object mass? Simply stated, they already figure out the role(s) of the object mass. As of now, the role is to perform Google searches, send text messages, open emails, use GPS, or watch viral videos on YouTube. This solidifies Baudrillard's claim of "obligatory consumption" in a "close system of models of signification."[563]

Musk's solution is Talking Heads' "fighting fire with fire" because we will still be "burning down the house." Former Googler Tristan Harris offers another "fighting fire with fire" solution on par with the oxymoron "business ethics" by asserting "The answer isn't to abandon technology. The answer is to change the technology industry to put our best interests first." Both Musk and Harris provide arguments similar to those made by pro-gun activists who generally claim "that guns don't kill people; people kill people."[564] In other words, the gun is perfectly fine. Keep the gun. Change the world. Keep the technology. Change the world. Just as the gun transformed humanity and its historical course, so does the advanced technology. To quote Harris, "we just need to keep going . . . [and] we will build machines that are smarter than we are . . . [and] they will improve themselves."[565] The inertial momentum of more guns and more gun violence parallels the more technology (AI) with more human irrelevancy. *WIRED* Journalist Olivia Solon declares "Sorry y'all, humanity's nearing an upgrade to irrelevance."[566] Her informal language exudes Harris's fun death by science fiction. It also illustrates the powerlessness of the object mass when confronted by technological utopians. Common language for common people. This "upgrade" to irrelevancy signals the total unawareness of the implications of human irrelevancy; or more accurately an awareness fueled by the residual stench of the Enlightenment. What is most striking is the total lack of any acknowledgement of the precedents laid down by previous technological advancement. The dream is in the absence. Cars without roads. Nuclear energy without the bomb. Plastic without litter. Tires without rubber. Baudrillard explains, "This is precisely where the crucial point lies, in the total misunderstanding on the part of the Enlightenment, of the relation between Good and Evil. We believe naively that the progress of Good, its advance in all fields (the sciences, technology . . .) corresponds to a defeat of Evil. No one seems to have understood that Good and Evil advance together, as part of the same movement."[567] Yet, Solon interviews Historian Yuval Harari, who appears to have a clear grasp on the irrelevancy of the human, but still resides in the utopian region of the "best-case scenario."

The *jouissance* or the excess of the good finds meaning in the personal and the collective. As noted previously, the excess of the good at the level of the individual involves convenience, instant knowledge, and constant consumption, connection, and entertainment. On the collective level, as cataloged with Google's inventions and charity, the good expands and grows globally. But to refer back to Baudrillard, "Good and Evil advance together."[568] Mander explains how the best-case scenarios dominate the conversation. In the case of Google, it is easy for the best-case scenario to dominate because the object mass engages with media through and by Google. Mander writes, "I have read . . . statements from scientists . . . at Lawrence Nuclear Laboratory, who develop weapons to save the 'free world'; computer scientists, who think advance computation can rid the world of toil and disease; satellite mappers, who seek to discover all the world's resources, and thereby end hunger. No one wants to believe he or she is engaged in something horrendous, so they seek to justify its imagined benefits."[569]

Solon asks Harari, "What can we be hopeful about?"[570] Harari responds, "There's a lot to be hopeful about. In 20 or 30 years, the hundreds of millions of people who have no health care will have access to AI doctors on their mobile phones [Android OS] offering better care than anyone gets now."[571] Harari's response illustrates the best-case scenarios attached to the prospects of the globe constructed by Google. Hundreds of millions of people without health care *will have mobile phones.* Advanced technology will resolve the health care debate. AI doctors *are* the health care of the future. But if we have AI doctors, why have organic humans? Why not have AI doctors who treat AI humans? Further, when asked if we can "opt out," Harari admits, "We might reach a point when it will be impossible to disconnect."[572] Baudrillard puts this into perspective. He writes, "The threshold of obligatory consumption can be set well above the strictly necessary . . . [and] the minimum of imposed consumption, is the standard package. Beneath this level, you are an outcast. Is loss of status, or social non-existence, less upsetting than hunger [or health care]?"[573] The mobile phone means (social) existence. Harari implies that advanced technology offers a future of where social existence takes precedence over health. The mobile phone is assumed while the access to health care is not. The mobile phone is obligatory consumption. But access to health care is not. This provides insight into the essence of the Google world. It is a world that offers internet access to refugees without addressing the creation of refugees. Finally, Harari mentions a "Dataist age"[574] where "meaning is generated by the external data processing system,"[575] and continues, "If you don't share your experiences [with your phone] they don't become part of the data processing system, and they have no meaning."[576] Social existence usurps physical existence or makes physical existence possible.

Physical existence does not occur without social existence through the mobile phone (Android OS). The paradox rests in the fact that all of the technological advancement results in the implosion of the object mass. With the implosion of the object mass comes the death of Google because no trace of humanity will be left to see it. Basically, the prisoners in Plato's *Cave* disappear and the shadows of AI that play against the wall have no more audience to participate.

One last vital point of human irrelevancy involves the conscious grasp of technological interaction. Žižek asks, "How will this affect our self-experience? Will we still experience ourselves as free beings or will we be regulated by digital machinery without being aware that we are regulated?"[577] This lack of conscious awareness of regulation by digital machinery further displaces the human from the world. Julian Assange explains how this occurs. He states: When you have AI programs harvesting all the search queries that people have on their phones and all the YouTube videos that human beings have uploaded it starts to lay out perceptual influence campaigns twenty to thirty moves ahead. This becomes totally beneath the level of human perception. And once a computer augmented organization, such as Google, is able to engage in influencing human beings twenty or thirty moves ahead, keeping each move beneath the level of human perception, there is nothing we can do about it because we cannot see it.[578]

Assange alludes to McLuhan's idea of technological invisibility. McLuhan writes, "Environments are not passive wrappings, but are, rather, active processes which are invisible. The ground rules, pervasive structure, and over-all patterns of environments elude easy perception."[579] The Google environment that initiates an algorithm that plans twenty to thirty moves ahead causes humans to be subject to the algorithm, but without any awareness of this subjection. Again, the irrelevancy of the human comes from the human that "keep[s] going."[580] Assange continues, "We are doomed because reality becomes something invisible and unperceivable . . . [and] we move towards a situation where human beings become irrelevant."[581] The attempt to reach complete comprehension of reality though human reason causes the most significant displacement of reality known to humankind. A displacement so destructive to all notions of reality that humankind can never know reality again. This is hyper-hyperreality. One practical example comes from Volkswagen. The BBC reports, "VW cars being sold in America had a 'defeat device,' or software, in diesel engines that could detect when they were being tested [for emissions], changing the performance accordingly to improve results."[582] This example shows the invisibility of technological function. Without human perception, a machine outsmarts another machine.

While this was declared a scandal, the normalized daily engagement with Google media is not scandalous, but functions the same way as the software in the Volkswagen. Essentially, the human will disappear without even noticing its disappearance; just like when the world ended in 1784 without anyone noticing. But unlike Morton's declaration of the end of the world, no human will be left to declare the end of humanity.

To conclude, Nietzsche asks the vital question that Google has answered. Nietzsche reflects, "Assuming . . . that we could not use any metaphysical explanations of the only world known to us, how would we then look upon men and things?"[583] The answer: Google will look upon men and things with the intent "to organize the world's information and make it universally accessible and useful"[584] All men and things are information to be used. To put it in Foucault's words, Google "supervises every instant . . . [and] compares, differentiates, hierarchizes, homogenizes, [and] excludes."[585]

In 1878, Nietzsche asks, "For according to historical probability, it is quite likely that men at some time will become skeptical about this whole subject of [metaphysics]. So one must ask the question: how will human society take shape under the influence of such an attitude?"[586] We now have the answer to Nietzsche's question; since 1878, because of the death of the metaphysical God and the advent of the scientific God, human society took the shape of a world mediated by applied science and advanced technology. It is a world that worships Google and all of its technological manifestations. Thus, we can now ask: how will human society take shape under the influence of an attitude skeptical about this whole subject of advanced technology and Google?

Notes

[1] Ludwig Andreas Feuerbach, *Lectures on the Essence of Religion* (Harper & Row, 1967), 187.
[2] Hans Küng, *Freud and the Problem of God* (Yale UP, 1979), 10.
[3] Ibid, 10.
[4] Daryl Ogdan, *The Language of the Eyes* (SUNY Press, 2005), 179.
[5] Charles Darwin, *The Descent of Man, and Selection in Relation to Sex* (D. Appleton, 1882), 591.
[6] C.G. Schoenfeld, "God the Father – And Mother: Study and Extension of Freud's Conception of God as an Exalted Father," *American Imago* 19 (1962): 215.
[7] Sigmund Freud, *Moses and Monotheism* (Hogarth Press, 1939), 18.
[8] Sigmund Freud, *Totem and Taboo*, 166.
[9] Ibid, 166.
[10] David Meghnagi and Mark Solms, *Freud and Judaism* (H. Karnec Books, 1993), 22
[11] Sigmund Freud, *Totem and Taboo*, 133.
[12] Ibid, 168.
[13] Jose Brunner, *Freud and the Politics of Psychoanalysis* (Transactions, 1999), 161.
[14] Sigmund Freud, *Moses and Monotheism*, 139.
[15] Sigmund Freud, *Civilization and its Discontents* (W.W. Norton, 1989), 107
[16] Sigmund Freud, *The Future of an Illusion*, 22.
[16] David Churchman, *Why We Fight: Theories of Human Aggression and Conflict* (UP of America, 2005), 272.
[17] Sigmund Freud, *The Interpretation of Dreams* (Basic Books, 2010), 278.

[18] Sigmund Freud, *The Freud Reader*, edited by Peter Gay (W.W. Norton, 1989), 640.
[19] Rachel Blass, "The Teaching of the Oedipus Complex: On Making Freud Meaningful to University Students by Unveiling to his Essential Ideas on the Human Condition," *The International Journal of Psychoanalysis* 82 (2001): 1112.
[20] Sigmund Freud, *The Freud Reader*, 640.
[21] Ibid, 641.
[22] Rachel Blass, "Teaching the Oedipus Complex," 1112.
[23] Ibid, 1113.
[24] C.G. Schoenfeld, "God the Father," 228.
[25] Naomi Morgenstern, "The Oedipus Complex made Simple," *U of Toronto Quarterly* 72 (2003): 780.
[26] Sigmund Freud, *Complete Works* (Ivan Smith, 2010), 1971.
[27] Rachel Blass, "Teaching the Oedipus Complex," 1114.
[28] Michael Kahn, *Basic Freud: Psychoanalytic Thought for the Twenty-First Century* (Basic Books, 2002), 87.
[29] Naomi Morgenstern, "The Oedipus Complex made Simple," 783.
[30] Michael Kahn, *Basic Freud: Psychoanalytic Thought for the Twenty-First Century*, 86-87.
[31] David Hume, *The Natural History of Religion* (Stanford UP, 1956), 30.
[32] C.G. Schoenfeld, "God the Father," 222.
[33] Ana-Marie Rizzuto, *The Birth of the Living God: A Psychoanalytic Study* (U of Chicago P, 1979), 209.
[34] Sigmund Freud, *The Future of an Illusion*, 49.
[35] Ibid, 30.
[36] Ibid, 31.

[37] Ibid, 30-31.
[38] Ibid, 31.
[39] Ibid, 31.
[40] Ibid, 17.
[41] Ibid, 18.
[42] Ibid, 19.
[43] Ibid, 19.
[44] Ibid, 19.
[45] Ibid, 10.
[46] Ibid, 23.
[47] Ibid, 23.
[48] Lorenzo Chiesa and Alberto Toscano, "Ethics and Capital, Ex Nihilio," *Umbr(a): The Dark God* (SUNY Buffalo P, 2005): 12.
[49] Tad Delay, *God is Unconscious: Psychoanalysis and Theology* (Wipf & Stock, 2015) 31.
[50] Jacques Lacan, *The Seminar of Jacques Lacan, Book VII. The Ethics of Psychoanalysis, 1959-1960* (W. W. Norton, 1992) 231.
[51] Clayton Crockett, "The Triumph of Tragedy." *Theology After Lacan: The Passion for the Real*, (Cascade Books, 2014): 230.
(qtd. in Delay)
[52] Ibid, 230.
[53] Jacques Lacan, *Seminar VII*, 74-75.
[54] Slavoj Žižek, "Why Only an Atheist Can Believe: Politics on the Edge of Fear and Trembling." *International Journal of Žižek Studies* (2007).
[55] Jacques Lacan, *On Feminine Sexuality: The Limits of Love and Knowledge, 1972-1973* (W.W. Norton & Company, 1975) 45.
[56] Michael Lewis, *Derrida and Lacan: Another Writing* (Edinburgh UP, 2008) 52.

[57] Ibid, 51
[58] James F. Anderson, *St. Augustine and Being,* 5.
[59] Clayton Crockett, "Triumph of Tragedy," 258.
[60] Augustine, *On the Trinity* (Catholic U American P, 1963), 441.
[61] Michael Lewis, *Derrida and Lacan: Another Writing*, 52.
[62] Boethius, *The Theological Tractates*, (G.P. Putnam's Sons, 1868), 57.
[63] Mary T. Clark, "De Trinitate," *The Cambridge Companion to Augustine* (Cambridge UP, 2005): 91-102.
[64] Adam Kotsko, *Žižek and Theology* (T & T Clark, 2008), 30.
[65] Jacques Lacan, *Seminar II*, 31.
[66] Dan Collins, "On Metaphor," *(Re)-Turn: A Journal of Lacanian Studies* 6 (2011): 149-158.
[67]Rex Butler, "Slavoj Žižek: What is a Master-Signifier," *Lacan.com* (2004) http://www.lacan.com/zizek-signifier.htm.
[68] Julian Wolfreys, *Critical Keywords in Literary and Cultural Theory* (Palgrave Macmillan, 2004), 108.
[69] Richard Boothby, Death and Desire: Psychoanalytic Theory in Lacan's Return to Freud (Routledge, 1991), 19.
[70] Julian Wolfreys, *Critical Keywords*, 108.
[71] Jacques Lacan, *Seminar III*, 63.
[72] Jacques Lacan, "The Mirror Stage as Formative of the Function of the I Revealed In Psychoanalytic Experience," (W.W. Norton & Company, 1975), 503.
[73] Aurelius Augustine, *The Works of Aurelius Augustine.: A New Translation. The City of God, Volume 2* (T. & T. Clark, 1872), 46
[74] Ibid, 517.
[75] Aurelius Augustine, *On Free Choice of the Will* (Hacknett Publishing, 1993), 25

[76] Stanislaus J. Grabowski, *The All-present God; a Study in St. Augustine* (B. Herder Books, 1954), 96.
[77] James F. Anderson, *St. Augustine and Being,* 5.
[78] "St. Augustine's Concept of God as the All-Present Being for the Present Generation," 48. http://catholic-church.org/grace/ecu/v/2.pdf.
[79] Ibid, 48.
[80] Stanislaus J. Grabowski, *All-present God*, 108.
[81] Ibid, 109.
[82] Aurelius Augustine, *The City of God Against the Pagans: Vol. 1*. (Cambridge UP, 1998), 452.
[83] Ibid, 452.
[84] Ibid, 200.
[85] Ibid, 201.
[86] Ibid, 202.
[87] Ibid, 204.
[88] Aurelius Augustine, *The Doctrinal Treatises of St. Augustine* (Jazzybee Verlag, 2012), 336.
[89] Ibid, 336.
[90] Aurelius Augustine, *Enchiridion* (SMK Books, 2015), 20.
[91] Ibid, 20.
[92] Anselm, *Proslogion* (Hacknett Publishing, 1995), 7
[93] Ibid, 8.
[94] Ibid, 10.
[95] Ibid, 11.
[96] Ibid, 22.
[97] Robert F. Brown, "Divine Omniscience, Immutability, Aseity and Human Free Will," *Religious Studies* 27 (1991): 280.
[98] Eileen Serene, "Anselm's Modal Conceptions," *Reforging the Great Chain of Being: Studies of the History*

of Modal Theories, edited by Simo Knuuttila, (D. Rediel, 1981): 141.

[99] Anselm, *Proslogium; Monologium; An Appendix in Behalf of the Fool by Gaunilon; and Cur Deus Homo*, (Open Court Publishing, 1926), 73.

[100] Ibid, 78.

[101] Ibid, 79. 126

[102] Ibid, 72.

[103] Hud Hudson, *The Fall and Hypertime*, (Oxford UP, 2014), 138.

[104] Anselm, *Proslogion*, 7.

[105] Thomas Aquinas, *Summa Theologica*, 188. http://www.basilica.org/pages/ebooks/St.%20Thomas%20 Aquinas-Summa%20Theologica.pdf.

[106] Ibid, 188.

[107] Ibid, 1562.

[108] Ibid, 188.

[109] Ibid, 186.

[110] Ibid, 195.

[111] Ibid, 729.

[112] Ibid, 356.

[113] Ibid, 728.

[114] Ibid, 356.

[115] Ibid, 97.

[116] Ibid, 98.

[117] Ibid, 101.

[118] Ibid, 101.

[119] Ibid, 103.

[120] Ibid, 106.

[121] Ibid, 156.

[122] Ibid, 156.

[123] Ibid, 156.
[124] Ibid, 156.
[125] Ibid, 29.
[126] Ibid, 38.
[127] Ibid, 38.
[128] Ibid, 38.
[129] James F. Anderson, *St. Augustine and Being*, 5.
[130] Friedrich Nietzsche, *The Complete Works of Friedrich Nietzsche* (Macmillan, 1924), 168.
[131] Mark Wrathall, "Introduction: Metaphysics and Onto-theology," *Religion After Metaphysics* (Cambridge UP, 2003): 1.
[132] Friedrich Nietzsche, *Complete Works*, 168.
[133] Robert Pippen, "Love and Death in Nietzsche," *Religion After Metaphysics* (Cambridge UP, 2003): 8.
[134] Andre Groenewald and Johan Buitendag, "Who is the 'God' Nietzsche Denied?" *Theological Studies* 61 (2005): 146. [192] Ibid, 147.
[135] Ibid, 147.
[136] Bernard Ramm, et. al. *"Is God "Dead?"* (Zondervan, 1966), 86.
[137] Andre Groenewald and Johan Buitendag, "Who is the 'God' Nietzsche Denied?" 147.
[138] Adrian Samuel, "Nietzsche and God (Part 1)," *Richmond Journal of Philosophy* 14 (2007): 2.
[139] Martin Heidegger, *The Question Concerning Technology and Other Essays*, (Garland Publishing, 1977), 71-72.
[140] Ibid, 74.
[141] Ibid, 74.
[142] Andre Groenewald and Johan Buitendag, "Who is the 'God' Nietzsche Denied?" 151.

[143] Michael Lackey, "Killing God, Liberating the 'Subject': Nietzsche and Post-God Freedom," *Journal of the History of Ideas* 60 (1999): 754.
[144] Friedrich Nietzsche, *Complete Works*, 168.
[145] Martin Heidegger, *Question Concerning Technology*, 61.
[146] Ernst Behlar, "Nietzsche in the Twentieth Century," *The Cambridge Companion to Nietzsche* (Cambridge UP, 1996), 314.
[147] Martin Heidegger, *Question Concerning Technology*, 66
[148] Ibid, 66.
[149] Friedrich Nietzsche, *The Birth of Tragedy and the Case of Wagner* (Vintage Books, 1967), 55.
[150] Rene Descartes, *A Discourse on Method* (E.P. Dutton, 1912), 32.
[151] Hans Küng, *Does God Exist?* (Knopf Doubleday, 2013), 17.
[152] Ibid, 18.
[153] Rene Descartes, *Meditations* (Bobbs-Merrill, 1960), 62.
[154] Rene Descartes, *Selected Philosophical Writings* (Cambridge UP, 1998), 165.
[155] Hans Küng, *Does God Exist?*, 36-37.
[156] Ezulike Benjamin Ofodile, "Kant on the Question of the Existence of God: From Destruction to Affirmation," *Iep.utm.edu*, http://www.ed1.ulg.ac.be/sd/textes
[157] Immanuel Kant, *Critique of Pure Reason* (Hacknett, 1987), 563.
[158] Ibid, 568.
[159] Ezulike Benjamin Ofodile, "Kant on the Question," 3.
[160] Alvin Plantinga, *God and Other Minds: A Study of the Rational Justification of Belief in God* (Cornell UP, 1967), 545.

[161] Ibid, 545.
[162] *Critique Pure Reason*, 571.
[163] Ibid, 572.
[164] Ezulike Benjamin Ofodile, "Kant on the Question," 6.
[165] *Critique Pure Reason*, 581.
[166] Friedrich Nietzsche, *Complete Works*, 168.
[167] Allen W. Wood, Kant's Rational Theology (Cornell UP, 1970), 62.
[168] Immanuel Kant, *Critique Pure Reason*, 607.
[169] Ibid, 607.
[170] Immanuel Kant, *Critique of Practical Reason* (Hacknett, 2002), 159.
[171] Andre Groenewald and Johan Buitendag, "Who is the 'God' Nietzsche Denied?" 152
[172] Immanuel Kant, *Critique of Judgment* (Hacknett, 1987), 339.
[173] John Caputo, "The Perversity of the Absolute, The Perverse Core of Hegel, and the Possibility of Radical Theology," *Hegel and the Infinite* (Columbia UP, 2011): 60.
[174] Joseph Prabhu, "Hegel's Secular Theology," *Sophia* 49 (2011): 222.
[175] Peter Hodgson, *Lectures on the Proofs of the Existence of God* (Clarendon Press, 2007), 15.
[176] J.A. Leighton, "Hegel's Conception of God," *The Philosophical Review* 5 (1896): 602.
[177] Ibid, 603.
[178] Thomas Altizer, *The Genesis of God: A Theological Genealogy* (Westminster / John Knox Press, 1993), 77.
[179] Richard Dien Winfield, "Hegel's Solution to the Mind-Body Problem," A Companion to Hegel (John Wiley &

Sons, 2011): 236.
[180] Darrel E. Christensen, "Hegel and a Doctrine of God for Theism," Indian Philosophical Quarterly 4 (1978): 527.
[181] Stephen R. C. Hicks, *Explaining Postmodernism*, 48
[182] Ibid, 48.
[183] Ibid, 48.
[184] Rustum Roy, "Religion/Technology, Not Theology/Science, as the Defining Dichotomy," *Zygon* 37 (2002): 667.
[185] Jacques Lacan, *The Seminar of Jacques Lacan, Book XI. The Four Fundamental Concepts of Psychoanalysis* (New York: W. W. Norton, 1978), 226.
[186] Alan G. Padgett, "God Versus Technology? Science, Secularity, And The Theology Of Technology," *Zygon* 40 (2005): 579.
[187] Ibid., 580-81.
[188] Lewis Mumford, *The Myth of the Machine*, 34.
[189] Ibid., 39.
[190] Ibid., 63.
[191] Ibid., 34.
[192] Friedrich Nietzsche, *Thus Spoke Zarathustra: A Book for All and None*. Translated by (Modern Library, 1995), 202.
[193] Ibid., 202.
[194] Babette Babich, "The Problem of Science of Science in Nietzsche and Heidegger," *Revista Portuguesa de Filosofia* (2007): 209.
[195] Roy, "Religion/Technology," 672.
[196] René Descartes, *A Discourse on Method* (E.P. Dutton, 1912), 49.
[197] Mumford, *The Myth of the Machine,* 82.
[198] Babich "The Problem of Science," 218.

[199] Martin Heidegger, *The Question Concerning Technology and Other Essays* (Garland Publishing, 1977), 64.
[200] Christopher May, "The Information Society as MegaMachine: The Continuing Relevance of Lewis Mumford," *Information, Communication and Society* 3 (2000): 247.
[201] Friedrich Nietzsche, *The Birth of Tragedy, and the Case of Wagner* (Vintage Books, 1967), 65.
[202] Adrian Samuel, "Nietzsche and God (Part 1)" *Richmond Journal of Philosophy* 14 (2007): 4-5.
[203] Gregory Morgan Swer, "Technics and (Para)Praxis: The Freudian Dimensions of Lewis Mumford's Theories of Technology," *History of the Human Sciences* 17 (2004): 59.
[204] Frank E. Manuel and Fritzie P. Manuel, *Utopian Thought in the Western World* (Belknap Press, 1979), 216.
[205] Swer, "Technics and (Para)Praxis," 59.
[206] Larry Stapleton, "Zarathustra and Beyond: Exploring Culture and Values Online," *AI and Society* 25 (2011): 97.
[207] Ibid., 97.
[208] Mumford, *The Myth of the Machine*, 72.
[209] Stapleton, "Zarathustra and Beyond," 98.
[210] Ibid., 98.
[211] Roy, "Religion/Technology," 670.
[212] Ibid., 673.
[213] Mumford, *The Myth of the* Machine," 66,70.
[214] Avron Kulak, "The Religious, the Secular, and the Natural Sciences: Nietzsche and the Death of God," *The European Legacy* 16 (2011): 792.
[215] Friedrich Nietzsche, *The Gay Science: With a Prelude in Rhymes and an Appendix of Songs* (Vintage Books, 1974), 283.

[216] Ibid., 179.
[217] William B. Drees, "Playing God? Yes! Religion in the Flight of Technology," *Zygon* (2002): 645.
[218] Ibid., 646.
[219] Mark E. Warren, "Nietzsche's Concept of Ideology," *Theory and Society* 13 (1984): 544.
[220] Virgilio Aquino Rivas, "The Death of God and Philosophy's Untimely Gospel," *Kritike*, 3 (2009): 144.
[221] Ibid., 145.
[222] Erling Hope, "Between God and Google: Reflections on the Technology Project of the Society for the Arts, Religion, and Contemporary Culture," *Crosscurrents* 62, (2012): 252.
[223] James F. Anderson, *St. Augustine and Being: A Metaphysical Essay* (Martinus Nijhoff, 1965).
[224] Ken Hillis et. al., *Google and the Culture of Search* (Routledge, 2013), 11.
[225] James Walters, *Baudrillard and Theology* (T & T Clark, 2012), 27.
[226] Jürgen Braungardt, "Theology After Lacan? A Psychoanalytic Approach to Theological Discourse," *Other Voices* 1 (1999): http://www.othervoices.org/1.3/jbraungardt/theology.php.
[227] Ibid.
[228] Lacan, *Seminar XI,* 27.
[229] Robert Epstein, "The New Censorship: How did Google become the Internet's Censor and Master Manipulator, Blocking Access to Millions of Websites?" *U.S. News and World Report*, June 22, 2016, http://www.usnews.com/opinion/articles/2016-06-22/google-is-the-worlds-biggestcensor-and-its-power-must-be-regulated.

[230] Jacques Lacan, *Écrits* (Routledge, 2001), 37-9.
[231] Jacques Lacan, *On the Names-of-the-Father* (Polity, 2015), 20.
[232] Ibid., 21.
[233] Tad Delay, *God is Unconscious: Psychoanalysis and Theology* (Wipf & Stock, 2015), 20-1.
[234] Ibid., 12.
[235] Marshall McLuhan, *Understanding Media* (McGraw-Hill, 1964), 19.
[236] Ibid., 51.
[237] Ibid., 51.
[238] Jean Baudrillard, *Seduction* (New World Perspectives, 1990), 166.
[239] Ibid., 167.
[240] Nicholas Carr, *The Shallows: What the Internet is Doing to Our Brains* (W.W. Norton, 2010), 48.
[241] Delay, *God Unconscious,* 9.
[242] Lacan, *Names Father*, 52.
[243] Sigmund Freud, *The Freud Reader* (W.W. Norton, 1989), 642.
[244] Delay, *God Unconscious*, 11.
[245] Jean Baudrillard, *Screened Out* (Verso 2002), 161.
[246] Jean Baudrillard, *Toward a Critique of the Political Economy of the Sign* (Telos Press, 1981), 169.
[247] Jacques Lacan, *The Seminar of Jacques Lacan, Book II. The Ego in Freud's Theory and in the Technique of Psychoanalysis, 1954-1955* (W. W. Norton, 1991), 38.
[248] Delay, *God Unconscious*, 13.
[249] Baudrillard, *Screened Out*, 161.
[250] Baudrillard, *Seduction*, 166)
[251] Marshall McLuhan, *Medium is the Massage* (Gingko

Press, 2001), 63.
[252] Hillis et. al., *Google Search*, 3.
[253] Ibid., 5.
[254] Ken Auletta, *Googled: The End of the World as we Know It* (Penguin, 2009), 8.
[255] Michel Foucault, *The Birth of Biopolitics* (Palgrave Macmillan, 2008), 67.
[256] See *World-Systems Analysis: An Introduction* by Immanuel Wallerstein for a further explanation. [314]
[257] These shifts are documented on https://moz.com/google-algorithm-change.
[258] Johnathan Edwards, *Sinners in the Hands of an Angry God and Other Puritan Sermons* (Dover, 2005), 177.
[259] Epstein, "New Censorship."
[260] Michel Foucault, *Discipline and Punish: The Birth of the Prison* (Vintage Books, 1995), 21.
[261] Auletta, *Googled*, 8.
[262] Jean Baudrillard, *Simulacra and Simulation* (U of Michigan P, 1995), 1.
[263] Foucault, *Discipline and Punish*, 202.
[264] Gerald Bray, "The Doctrine of the Trinity in Augustine's De Civitate Dei," *European Journal of Theology* 1 (1992): 146.
[265] Ibid., 145.
[266] Ibid., 145.
[267] The new motto for Alphabet Inc., Google's holding company since October 2015, is "Do the Right Thing;" See *Wall Street Journal*, October 2, 2015 article "Google's 'Don't Be Evil' Becomes Alphabet's 'Do the Right Thing'" by Alistair Barr.
[268] Augustine, *On Free Choice of the Will* (Hacknett Publishing, 1993), 8-12.

[269] Antal van den Bosch, et. al., "Estimating Search Engine Index Size Variability: A 9-year Longitudinal Study," *Scientometrics* (2016) http://www.dekunder.nl/Media/10.1007_s11192-016-1863-z.pdf.
[270] Nicholas Carr, *The Big Switch: Rewiring the World, From Edison to Google* (W. W. Norton, 2008), 41.
[271] Auletta, *Googled*, 8.
[272] Hillis et. al., *Google Search*, 53.
[273] Delay, *God Unconscious*, 12.
[274] Thomas Aquinas, *Summa Theologica* (1485), 188. http://www.basilica.org/pages/ebooks/St.%20Thomas%20AquinasSumma%20Theologica.pdf.
[275] Epstein, "New Censorship."
[276] Ibid.
[277] Thomas, *Summa*, 2694.
[278] Shadia B. Drury, *Terror and Civilization: Christianity, Politics, and The Western Psyche* (Palgrave Macmillan, 2004), 26.
[279] Hillis et. al., *Google Search*, 14.
[280] See *Google and the Culture of Search* by Hillis et. al. pages 146-176; *The Google Story* by Vise, pages 98-98; *In the Plex* by Levy, pages 460462; *The Googlization of Everything* by Vaidhyanathan, pages 156-173.
[281] "Google Library Project." Google Books, accessed August 10, 2016, https://books.google.com/googlebooks/library/.
[282] J.A. Leighton, "Hegel's Conception of God," *The Philosophical Review* 5 (1896): 617-8.
[283] Stephen R. C. Hicks, *Explaining Postmodernism*, 47.
[284] David Vise, *The Google Story*. (Pan Macmillan Books,

2006), 60.
[285] Ibid., 60.
[286] Jean Baudrillard, *In the Shadow of the Silent Majorities* (Semiotext(e), 1983), 5, 22, 30.
[287] Geeksquad, "The Best Free Email Services" January 7, 2016, http://www.geeksquad.co.uk/articles/best-free-email-services. Accessed on June 17, 2016.
[288] See https://www.google.com/intl/en/policies/privacy/.
[289] Auletta, *Googled*, 62.
[290] Ibid., 62.
[291] Steven Levy, *In the Plex: How Google Thinks, Works, and Shapes our Lives* (Simon and Shuster, 2011), 170.
[292] Laura Northrup, "Google Will Stop Data-Mining Student E-Mail Accounts," *Consumerist,* April 30, 2014, https://consumerist.com/2014/04/30/google-will-stop-data-mining-student-e-mail-accounts/.
[293] Herold Benjamin, "Google Under Fire for Data-Mining Student Email Messages,"
Education Week, March 13, 2014,
http://edweek.org/ew/articles/2014/03/13/ 26google.h33.html
[294] Epstein, "New Censorship."
[295] Chris Morran, "College Students Sue Google for Scanning School-Issued Gmail Accounts," *Consumerist*, February 3, 2016, https://consumerist.com/2016/02/03/college-students-sue-google-for-scanning-school-issued-gmail-accounts/.
[296] Jackie Smith and Alfredo Lopez. "Let's Stop Google from Gobbling Up our Schools." *Counterpunch*, June 3, 2016, http://www.counterpunch.org/2016/06/03/lets-stop-google-from-gobbling-up-our-schools/.
[297] Ibid.
[298] Ibid.

[299] See Ellen Nakashima, "Google to Enlist NSA to Ward Off Attacks; Firm Won't Share User Data, Sources Say, But Deal Raises Issue of Privacy vs. Security," *Washington Post*, February 4, 2010.
[300] Jerry Mander, *The Case Against the Global Economy: And for a Turn Towards Localization* (Earthscan from Routledge, 2001), 47.
[301] Augustine, *The Works of Aurelius Augustine.: A New Translation. The City of God, Volume 2*, (T. & T. Clark, 1872), 174.
[302] Anselm, *Proslogion* (Hacknett Publishing, 1995), 7.
[303] Augustine, *Enchiridion*, (SMK Books, 2015), 20.
[304] Alex Kuskis, "We Shape Our Tools and Thereafter Our Tools Shape Us." *McLuhan Galaxy*, April 1, 2013, https://mcluhangalaxy.wordpress.com/2013/ 04/01/we-shape-our-tools-and-thereafter-our-tools-shape-us/.
[305] B.J. Mendalson, "Social Media is Bullshit Presentation." *YouTube*, uploaded by blosintobook, November 8, 2013, https://www.youtube.com/watch?v=-W8fp5pyveU.
[306] Levy, *In the Plex*, 385.
[307] Mike Gane, *Baudrillard (RLE Social Theory): Critical and Fatal Theory* (Routledge, 1991), 141. [364]
[308] Ibid., 141.
[309] Slavoj Žižek, *How to Read Lacan* (W.W. Norton, 2006), 12.
[310] Jean Baudrillard, *Consumer Society* (Sage, 1998), 87.
[311] Ibid., 89.
[312] Noam Chomsky, *The Common Good* (Odonian Press, 1998), 43.
[313] Steven Harris, "Žižek on 'Forced Choice,'" *Theological Journey*, December 26, 2009, https://stevenedwardharris.com/2009/12/26/zizek-

on%E2%80%9Cforced choice%E2%80%9D/.
[314] Siva Vaidhyanathan, *The Googlization of Everything (And Why We Should Worry)* (U of California P, 2011), 200.
[315] Slavoj Žižek, *The Sublime Object of Ideology* (Verso, 1989), 165.
[316] Jeff Pruchnic, "Fistful of Žižek," *Untimely Mediations*, April 13, 2008, https://untimelymediations.wordpress.com/category/zizek/.
[317] Slavoj Žižek, *The Plague of Fantasies* (Verso, 1997), 29.
[318] Ibid., 29.
[319] Vaidhyanathan, *Googlization*, 7.
[320] Holman W. Jenkins Jr., "Google and the Search for the Future," *Wall Street Journal*, August 14, 2010, http://www.wsj.com/articles/SB1000142405274870490110 4575423 294099527212.
[321] Baudrillard, *Simulacra and Simulation*, 31.
[322] Ibid., 31
[323] Ibid., 29.
[324] Vaidhyanathan, *Googlization*, 200.
[325] Hillis et. al., *Google Search*, 202.
[326] Ibid., 202.
[327] Jean-Noël Jeanneney, *Google and the Myth of Universal Knowledge: A View from Europe* (U of Chicago P, 2007), 73.
[328] Auletta, *Googled*, 13.
[329] Levy, *In the Plex*, 351.
[330] Ibid., 352.
[331] Ibid., 358, 361.
[332] Hillis et. al., *Google Search*, 170.

[333] Vise, *Google Story*, 28.
[334] Ibid., 203-1.
[335] John Battelle, *The Search: How Google and Its Rivals Rewrote the Rules of Business and Transformed our Culture* (Portfolio, 2006), 210.
[336] Luther, Martin, "Disputation Concerning Man," *Universitat Duisberg-Essen*, https://www.unidue.de/collcart/es/sem/s6/txt12_1.htm.
[337] Ibid.
[338] Vise, Google Story, 278.
[339] See the article from January 2016, "Why Google Quit China, and Why It's Heading Back" by Kaveh Waddell.
[340] Kaveh Waddell, "Why Google Quit China, and Why It's Heading Back," *The Atlantic*, January 19, 2016. http://www.theatlantic.com/technology/archive/2016/01/why-google-quit-china-and-why-its-heading-back/424482/.
[341] Nicholas D. Kristof, "Could Google Bring Freedom to China?," *New York Times*, April 5, 2001, 12.
[342] Ibid., 13.
[343] Battelle, *Google Rewrote*, 66.
[344] Ibid., 66.
[345] Adrian Peter Tse, "China's Google Ban Gives Baidu Search Engine Global Boost," *Campaign*, April 2, 2015, http://www.campaignlive.com/article/chinas-google-ban-gives-baidu- search-engine-global-boost/1341336.
[346] Anselm, *Proslogion*, 11.
[347] See "Google Foundation" at http://www.insidephilanthropy. com/grants-for-global-development/google-foundation-grants-for-globaldevelopment.html.
[348] See "Google Impact Challenge" at https://www.google.org/ impactchallenge/disabilities/.

[349] Ibid.

[350] "Mission Arm," Google.org, accessed August 24, 2016, https://www.google.org/impactchallenge/disabilities/grantees/mission-arm.html.

[351] "Miraclefeet," Google.org, accessed August 24, 2016, https://www.google.org/impactchallenge/disabilities/grantees/miraclefeet.html.

[352] "Leprosy Mission," accessed August 24, 2016, https://www.google.org/impactchallenge/disabilities/grantees/ leprosy-mission-trust.html.

[353] See the following Bible verses to compare Google activities with those of God the Son: 1) John 5:6-18 explains that God the Son heals the lame and, more profoundly, does so on the Sabbath; thereby, God the Son broke the law of the Sabbath, but He can break laws and make new laws for the good of the human. 2) Matthew 8:1-3 relates how God the Son heals the leper.

[354] Donna Callejon. "Google Hunger Relief Campaign: Simple Ways to Take a Bite out of Hunger," *Global Goodness*, January 13, 2013, http://blog.globalgivingorg/2013/01/10/ google-hunger-relief-campaign-simple-ways-to-take-a-bite-out-of-hunger/.

[355] Ibid.

[356] Ibid.

[357] Matthew 1:13-21 describes how God the Son fed "about five thousand men, besides women and children" (*New International Version*).

[358] Callejon, "Google Hunger Relief,"

[359] Ibid.

[360] Ibid.

[361] "Google Special Programs," accessed August 24, 2016, https://www.google.org/special-programs/.

[362] Roland Barthes, *Mythologies.* (Hill and Wang, 2013), 186.
[363] "NetHope," http://nethope.org. Accessed on Auguste 24, 2016.
[364] Ibid.

[365] Anna Bawden, "Google's Charitable Chief: 'I Have a Strong Sense of Social Justice,'" *The Guardian*, July 22, 2015, https://www.theguardian.com/society/2015 /jul/22/ googleorg-charitable-chief-jacquelline-fuller-100m-fund--social-justice.
[366] See Mark 8:22-26.
[367] See Mark 8:34 in the *King James Version.*
[368] For more information on "Google Fiber," see https://fiber.google.com/about/.
[369] Issie Lapowsky, "Google is Bringing Free Gigabit Fiber to Public Housing Across the US," *WIRED*, February 3, 2016, https://www.WIRED.com/2016/02/google-is-bringing-free-gigabit-fiber-to-public-housing-across-the-us/.
[370] Ibid.

[371] Alezandra Mosher, "Google Helps Kids Send Videos to Dads in Prison on Father's Day," *USA Today*, June 18, 2016,
http://www.usatoday.com/story/tech/news/2016/06/18/ google-helps-kids-send-videos-dads-prison-fathersday/86050458
[372] Anselm, *Proslogion*, 11.
[373] "Google Impact Challenge."

[374] Davey Alba, "Google.org Thinks it Can Engineer a Solution to the World's Woes," *WIRED*, March 8, 2016, https://www.WIRED.com/2016/03/giving-google-way/.
[375] Robert F. Brown, "Divine Omniscience, Immutability, Aseity and Human Free Will." *Religious Studies* 27

(1991): 285.
[376] Thomas, Summa, 106.
[377] See https://www.google.com/edu/case-studies/ to read case studies from institutions that "benefitted" from "Google Apps for Education."
[378] Daryl Y. Mendoza, "Commodity, Sign, and Spectacle: Retracing Baudrillard's Hyperreality," *Kritike* 4 (2010): 48.
[379] Ibid., 48.
[380] Baudrillard, *Silent Majorities*, 30.
[381] Baudrillard, *Consumer Society*, 88.
[382] Ibid., 87
[383] Issie, Lapowsky, "Google Wants to Save Our Schools and Hook a New Generation of Users," *WIRED*, August 13, 2014, https://www.WIRED.com/2014/08/google-classrooms/.
[384] Ibid.
[385] Anya Kamenetz, "What Do Schools Risk by Going 'Full Google,'" *KQED News*, August 28, 2014, https://ww2.kqed.org/mindshift/2014/08/28/what-do-schools-risk-by-going-full-google/.
[386] Ibid.
[387] "G Suite Terms of Service," Google.com, Accessed on August 17, 2016, https://gsuite.google.com/terms/user_terms .html.
[388] Foucault, *Discipline and Punish*, 201.
[389] Ibid., 21.
[390] Baudrillard, *Simulacra and Simulation*, 29.
[391] Ibid., 31.
[392] Kamenetz, "Schools Risk."
[393] "About Android," Developer.android.com, accessed on

August 15, 2016, https://developer.android.com/about/android.html.
[394] Simon Hill, "Google Photos: Should You Be Worried About Privacy," *Android Authority*, June 16, 2015, http://www.androidauthority.com/google-photos-worried-privacy-616339/.
[395] Ibid.
[396] Damon Beres, "Even If You Uninstall Google Photos, It Will Keep Uploading Your Pics," *The Huffington Post*, July 13, 2015, http://www.huffingtonpost.com/entry/google-photos-will-upload-your-pics-to-the-cloud-even-if-you-uninstall-the-app_us_55a 3eecbe4b0b8145f731be2.
[397] Ibid.
[398] *King James Version.*
[399] Marshall McLuhan, *Counterblast* (Rapp & Whiting, 1970), 132.
[400] "Google Pattern Recognition," Google.com/polocies, accessed on August 29, 2016, https://www.google.com/policies/technologies/patternrecognition/.
[401] Ibid.
[402] Melonie S. Wright, "Face It: Snapchat, Facebook, and Google Dealing with Suits Over Facial Recognition Technology," *Mondaq*, September 19, 2016, http://www.mondaq.com /unitedstates/x/527964/.
[403] Guy Debord, *The Society of the Spectacle* (Zone Books, 1994), 4.
[404] Baudrillard, *Simulacra and Simulation*, 100.
[405] Ibid., 100.
[406] David A. Arnott, "Google Photos May Be Uploading your Pics, Even if You Don't Want It To," *Upstart*, July 10, 2015,

http://upstart.bizjournals.com/news/technology/2015/07/10/google-photos-uploads-images-without-app.html?page=4.

[407] Baudrillard, *Simulacra and Simulation*, 102.

[408] "Google Privacy & Terms," accessed on September 10, 2016, Google.com, https://www.google.com/intl/en/policies/.

[409] Ibid.

[410] Chris B. Hoffman, "How to Train Siri, Cortana, and Google to Understand Your Voice Better," *How-To Geek,* October 18, 2015, http://www.howtogeek.com/231329/how-to-train-siri-cortana-and-google-to-understand-your-voice-better/.

[411] Robert McMillan, "How Google Retooled Android with Help from Your Brain," *WIRED*, February 18, 2013, https://www.WIRED.com/2013/02/android-neural-network/.

[412] Carr, *The Shallows*, 25.

[413] McMillan, "Google Retooled."

[414] Andrew Griffin, "Google Voice Search Record and Keeps Conversations People Have Around Their Phones," *Independent*, June 1, 2016, http://www.independent.co.uk/life-style/gadgets-and-tech/news/

[415] Ibid.

[416] Rick Falkvinge, "So Google Records All the Microphone Audio All the Time, After All?" *Privacy News Online*, October 30, 2015. https://www.privateinternetaccess.com/blog/ 2015/10/so-google-records-all-the-microphone-audio-all-the-time-after-all/.

[417] "Google Self-Driving Car," Google.com, accessed on September 10, 2016, https://www.google.com/selfdrivingcar /faq/#q2

[418] Ibid.
[419] Ibid.
[420] Joe Hindy, "Ten Best GPS App and Navigation App Options for Android," *Android Authority*, April 14, 2016, http://www.androidauthority.com/best-gps-app-and-navigation-app-for-android-357870/.
[421] "Google Play Maps App," Play.google.com, accessed on September 11, 2016, https://play.google.com/store/apps /details?id=com.google.android.apps.maps&hl=en.
[422] James Ball, "Angry Birds and 'Leaky' Phone Apps Targeted by NSA and GCHQ for User Data," *The Guardian*, January 28, 2014, https://www.theguardian.com/world/2014 /jan/27/nsa-gchq-smartphone-app-angry-birds-personal-data.
[423] Marshall McLuhan, *From Cliché to Archetype* (Viking Press, 1970), 9.
[424] "Google Maps," Google.com, accessed on September 10, 2016 https://www.google.com/maps/about/.
[425] Eric Schmidt and Jonathan Rosenberg, *How Google Works* (Grand Central Publishing, 2014), 201.
[426] Ibid., 201.
[427] David Kushner, "A Home at the End of Google Earth," *Vanity Fair*, October 8, 2012, http://www.vanityfair.com/culture/2012/11/indiaorphan-google-earth-journey.
[428] Ibid.
[429] Cade Metz, "Paired with AI and VR, Google Earth Will Change the Planet," *WIRED*, June 29, 2015, http://www.WIRED.com/2015/06/pairedai-vr-google-earth-will-change-planet/#article-comments.
[430] Ibid.
[431] Ibid.
[432] "Google Earth," Google.com, accessed September 10,

2016, https://www.google.com/earth/explore/products/.

[433] Metz, "Google Earth" 2015.

[434] Ibid.

[435] Napier Lopez, "Google's Satellites Will Now Do Much More than Just Update Your Maps," *The Next Web*, March 8, 2016, http://thenextweb.com/google/2016/03/08/google-rebrands-satellite-imaging-company-terra-bella/#gref.

[436] "Terra Bella," Google.com, accessed on September 23, 2016, https://terrabella.google.com/.

[437] Ibid.

[438] Ibid.

[439] Ibid.

[440] Ibid.

[441] Daniel Van Boom, "Google's Magic Internet Balloons Bringing Wi-Fi to India," *C-Net*, March 6, 2016, https://www.cnet.com/news/googlesmagic-internet-balloons-bringing-wi-fi-to-india/.

[442] "Google Project Loon," *X.company*, https://x.company/loon/.

[443] Ibid.

[444] Van Boom, "Magic Balloon."

[445] Surabhi Agarwal, "Google May Get Government Nod to Conduct Pilot for Project Loon in India," *Economic Times*, May 24, 2016, http://economictimes.indiatimes.com/ tech/internet/google-may-get-government-nod-to-conduct-pilot-for-project-loon-inindia/articleshow/52408455.cms.

[446] Data from "2015 Search Engine Market Share by Country" from *Return on Now*, www.returnonnow.com/internet-marketing-resources/2015search-engine-market-share-by-country/.

[447] "Google Project Wing," *X.company*, https://x.company/projects/wing/, Accessed on September 24, 2016.
[448] Ibid.
[449] Matt McFarland, "Google Drones Will Deliver Chipotle Burritos at Virginia Tech," *CNN Tech*, September 8, 2016, http://money.cnn.com/2016/09/08/technology/google-drone-chipotle-burrito/.
[450] Ibid.
[451] Alexis C. Madrigal, "Inside Google's Secret Drone-Delivery Program," *The Atlantic*, August 28, 2014, http://www.theatlantic.com/technology/archive/2014/08/inside-googles-secret-drone-delivery-program/379306/.
[452] Oliver Burkeman, "Death, Drones, and Driverless Cars: How Google Wants to Control our Lives," *The Guardian*, September 22, 2014, https://www.theguardian.com/technology/2014/sep/22/what-does-google-want-glass-drones-self-driving-cars.
[453] Mike Murphy's article, "Google Wants to have Drones Buzzing around Offices, projecting our Faces at Meetings" provides information on other uses related to the drones.
[454] "Google Daydream," Vr.google.com, accessed on September 15, 2016, https://vr.google.com/daydream/.
[455] Ibid.
[456] Žižek, Sublime Object, 186.
[457] "Google Daydream"
[458] Ross Inman, "Omnipresence and the Location of the Immaterial," *Oxford Studies in Philosophy And Religion* 7 (2014): 4.
[459] Thomas, *Summa*, 729.
[460] McLuhan, *Medium Massage*, 69.
[461] Jerry Mander, *In the Absence of the Sacred* (Sierra

Club Books, 1992), 31.
[462] Ibid., 32.
[463] Ibid., 31.
[464] Jean Baudrillard, *Political Economy of the Sign*, 176.
[465] Ibid., 176.
[466] Peter Dallow, "The Space of Information: Digital Media as Simulation of the Analogical Sign," *Technospaces*, edited by Sally Munt, Continuum, (2001): 57.
[467] Ibid., 57.
[468] Ibid., 57.
[469] Foucault, *Discipline and Punish*, 232.
[470] Ibid., 214.
[471] The full quote reads: "Reports that say that something hasn't happened are always interesting to me, because as we know, there are known knowns; there are things we know we know. We also know there are known unknowns; that is to say we know there are some things we do not know. But there are also unknown unknowns, the ones we don't know we don't know. And if one looks throughout the history of our country and other free countries, it is the latter category that tend to be the difficult ones" (Rumsfeld).
[472] Slavoj Žižek, "What Rumsfeld Doesn't Know that He Knows About Abu Gharib," *In These Times*, May 21, 2004, http://inthesetimes.com/article/747/what_rumsfeld_doesn_know_that_he_knows_about_abu_ghraib.
[473] Slavoj Žižek, "Between Two Deaths: The Culture of Torture," *Lacan.com*, 3 Jun. 2004, http://www.lacan.com/zizektorture.htm
[474] Delay, *God Unconscious*, 12.

[475] "Consortium for the Barcode of Life," Google.org, accessed on October 15, 2016, https://www.google.org/global-giving/global-impactawards/cbol/.
[476] Ibid.
[477] Daniel Tutt, "Instituting Lack and Traversing Fantasy in the New Discourse on Tolerance," *DanielTutt.com*, 17 Nov. 2009, https://danieltutt.com/2009/11/17/instituting-lack-and-traversing-fantasy-in-the-new-discourse-on-tolerance/.
[478] Ibid.
[479] "And out of the ground the LORD God formed every beast of the field, and every fowl of the air; and brought *them* unto Adam to see what he would call them: and whatsoever Adam called every living creature that *was* the name thereof. And Adam gave names to all cattle, and to the fowl of the air, and to every beast of the field" (*King James Version*, Genesis 2:19-20).
[480] Tutt, "Instituting Lack."
[481] Simon Swift, *Hannah Arendt* (Routledge, 2009), 110.
[482] Žižek, "Rumsfeld."
[483] *Google Nexus 7 Commercial (Fearless)*, YouTube video, 1:10, uploaded by "BMS," August 25, 2013, https://www.youtube.com/watch?v=mH9QEz0TF1s.
[484] Ibid.
[485] Sara Beardsworth, *Julia Kristeva: Psychoanalysis and Modernity* (SUNY New York P, 2004), 43.
[486] Jacques Lacan, *The Seminar of Jacques Lacan, Book III. The Psychoses, 1955-56.* (W. W. Norton, 1993), 319.
[487] Ibid.
[488] *Introducing Google Home*, YouTube video, 1:14, uploaded by "Google," October 4, 2016,

https://www.youtube.com/watch?v=r0iLfAV0pIg.
[489] Sharon Gaudin, "How Google Home's 'Always On' Will Affect Privacy," *Computerworld*, October 6, 2016, http://www.computerworld.com/article/3128791/data-privacy/how-google-homes-always-on-will-affect-privacy.html.
[490] Ibid.
[491] Ibid.
[492] Lacan, *Écrits*, 1-2.
493 Sigmund Freud, Complete Works, 2934, http://archive.org/stream /TheCompleteWorksOf SigmundFreud/ebooksclub.org __Freud___Complete_works _djvu.txt.
[494] Lacan, *Écrits*, 2.
[495] André Nusselder, *Interface Fantasy: A Lacanian Cyborg Ontology* (MIT P, 2009), 84.
[496] Ibid., 85.
[497] *Google App TV Commercial, Dreams*, Ispot.tv, https://www.ispot.tv/ad/7Mal/ google-app-Dreams.
[498] Lacan, *Seminar XI*, 224.
[499] Ibid., 224.
[500] Ibid., 224.
[501] "Google Company Mission," https://www.google.com/about/company/, Accessed on August 27, 2016.
[502] Nusselder, *Interface Fantasy*, 115
[503] Lacan, *Seminar XI*, 232.
[504] Nusselder, *Interface Fantasy*, 115.
[505] *The Google App: Questions*, YouTube video, 1:00, uploaded by "Google," May 3, 2015, https://www.youtube.com/watch?v=5shykyfmb28.
[506] Lacan, *Seminar XI*, 225.

[507] *Google Home TV Commercial, Blue Whale*, YouTube video, 0:30, posted by "Corey Devonacha," November 27, 2016, https://www.youtube.com/watch?v=e__-7pSHOqc.
[508] Baudrillard, *Simulacra and Simulation*, 6.
[509] Ibid., 1.
[510] Ibid., 4.
[511] *Meet Your Google Assistant, Your Own Personal Google,* YouTube video, 1:36, posted by "Google," October 4, 2016, https://www.youtube.com/watch?v=FPfQMVf4vwQ.
[512] Obviously, the reference to the Depeche Mode song, "Personal Jesus" comes to mind. The lyrics read, "Your own personal Jesus. Someone to hear your prayers. Someone who's there" (Depeche Mode).
[513] Vaidhyanathan, *Googlization*, 200.
[514] Jean Baudrillard, *The Agony of Power* (Semiotext(e), 2010), 79-80.
[515] Jason Cipriani and Vanessa Hand Orellana, "Google Assistant: Tips for Talking to Pixel, Google Home and Allo." *Cnet*, November 3, 2016, https://www.cnet.com/how-to/google-assistant-tips-commands-pixel-google-home-allo/.
[516] Baudrillard, *Agony Power*, 81.
[517] Eric Schmidt and Jared Cohen, *The New Digital Age* (Alfred A. Knopf, 2013), 1.
[518] Jean Baudrillard, *Silent Majorities*, 2.
[519] Jean Baudrillard, *Fatal Strategies* (Semiotext(e), 1990), 32.
[520] *Metropolis*, directed by Fritz Lang (Unversum Film AG, 1927).
[521] *BBC News*, "Smartphone Use in Restaurants Prompts Craigslist Rant," July 14, 2014,

http://www.bbc.com/news/blogs-echochambers28272380.
[522] *Thailand Business News*, "80% of Population Aged 25-34 in Thailand Own Smartphones," December 20, 2014, https://www.thailandbusiness-news.com/lifestyle/
[523] Young Persons University of Manchester, "Turn that Fomo Upside Down," August 25, 2016, http://www.ypu.manchester.ac.uk/blog/turn-thatfomo-upside-down.
[524] Jean Baudillard, *Consumer Society*, 155.
[525] Ibid, 156.
[526] Jean Baudrillard, *Agony of Power*, 79.
[527] Ibid, 59.
[528] Ibid, 60.
[529] Jean Baudrillard, *Agony of Power*, 79.
[530] Ibid.
[531] Tad Delay, *God is Unconscious*, 30.
[532] Ibid, 32.
[533] Slavoj Zizek, *Zizek's Jokes* (MIT UP, 2014), 47.
[534] Jean Baudrillard, *America* (Verso, 1988), 30.
[535] Marshall McLuhan and Eric McLuhan, *Laws of Media: The New Science* (U of Toronto P, 1992).
[536] Jean Baudrillard, *America*, 32.
[537] Jean Baudrillard, *Political Economy of the Sign*, 169.
[538] Jean Baudrillard, *Agony of Power*, 84.
[539] Jean Baudrillard, *Why Hasn't Everything Already Disappeared?* (Seagull, 2011), 34.
[540] Aaron Souppouris, "Artificial Intelligence Learns Mario Level in Just 34 Attempts," June 17, 2015, https://www.engadget.com/2015/06/17/ super-mario-world-self-learning-ai/.
[541] Jean Baudrillard, *Everything Disappeared*, 34.
[542] *McLuhan's Wake*, directed by Kevin McMahon and David Sobelman. (Disinformation, 1993).

[543] Jean Baudrillard, *Fatal Strategies*, 49
[544] Ibid, 30.
[545] Jean Baudrillard, *Agony of Power*, 85.
[546] Jean Baudrillard, *Everything Disappeared*, 34.
[547] Timothy Morton, *Hyperobjects: Philosophy and Ecology After the End of the World* (U of Minnesota P, 2013), 10.
[548] Ibid, 14.
[549] Talking Heads, "Once in a Lifetime," *Remain in Light*, Sire, 1980.
[550] Jean Baudrillard, *Agony of Power*, 87.
[551] Ibid, 86.
[552] Ibid, 86.
[553] Talking Heads "Burning Down the House," *Speaking in Tongues*, Sire, 1983.
[554] Marshall McLuhan, *Medium Massage*, 79.
[555] Jean Baudrillard, *Silent Majorities*, 22.
[556] *Can we Build AI Without Losing Control Over It? Sam Harris*, YouTube video, 14:27, posted by "TED," October 19, 2016, https://www.youtube.com/watch?v=8nt3edWLgIg.
[557] Ibid.
[558] Ibid.
[559] Andrew J. Hawkins, "Elon Musk Thinks Humans Need to Become Cyborgs or Risk Irrelevance," *The Verge*, February 13, 2017, https://www.theverge.com/2017/2/13/14597434/elon-musk-human-machine-symbiosis-self-driving-cars.
[560] Ibid.
[561] *Slavoj Žižek on Artificial Intelligence*, YouTube video, 11:07, posted by "The Žižek Times," May 7, 2017, https://www.youtube.com/watch?v=kh32E6O4K0k.

[562] Andrew J. Hawkins, "Elon Musk Thinks," *The Verge.*
[563] Jean Baudrillard, *Political Economy of the Sign*, 81, 175.
[564] *Timewellspent.io*, accessed August 5, 2017, http://timewellspent.io.
[565] *Can we Control AI? Sam Harris*, "TED."
[566] Olivia Solon, "Sorry, Y'all, Humanity's Nearing an Upgrade to Irrelevance," *WIRED*, February 21, 2017, https://www.wired.com/2017/02/yuval-harari-tech-is-the-new-religion/.
[567] Jean Baudrillard, *The Spirit of Terrorism* (Verso, 2002), 13.
[568] Ibid, 13.
[569] Jerry Mander, *Absence Sacred*, 165.
[570] Olivia Solon, "Upgrade to Irrelevance," *WIRED.*
[571] Ibid.
[572] Ibid.
[573] Jean Baudrillard, *Political Economy of the Sign*, 81.
[574] Olivia Solon, "Upgrade to Irrelevance," *WIRED.*
[575] Ibid.
[576] Ibid.
[577] *Slavoj Žižek on Artificial Intelligence*, "The Žižek Times."
[578] *[NEW VIDEO] Žižek, Assange & M.I.A. on AI Controlled Social Media at Meltdown Festival*, YouTube video, 28:16, posted by "The Žižek Times," June 12, 2017, https://www.youtube.com/watch?v=HVkMX4p1kpI.
[579] McLuhan, *Medium Massage*, 69.
[580] *Can we Control AI? Sam Harris*, "TED."
[581] *Žižek, Assange & M.I.A. on AI*, "The Žižek Time."
[582] Russell Hotten, "Volkswagen: The Scandal Explained,"

BBC, December 10, 2015,
http://www.bbc.com/news/business-34324772.
583 Friedrich Nietzsche, *Human, All too Human* (Wildside, 2011), 38.
584 "Google Company Mission,"
https://www.google.com/about/company/.
585 Michel Foucault, *Discipline and Punish*, 183.
586 Friedrich Nietzsche, *Human, all Too Human*, 38.

89449830R00146

Made in the USA
San Bernardino, CA
25 September 2018